Called 2 Love

A 40-Day Journey into Marriage Intimacy

Dr. David and Teresa Ferguson
Steve and Barbara Uhlmann

BroadStreet
P U B L I S H I N G

BroadStreet Publishing® Group, LLC
Savage, Minnesota, USA
BroadStreetPublishing.com

Called 2 Love: A 40-Day Journey into Marriage Intimacy

978-1-4245-5792-9 (softcover)
978-1-4245-5793-6 (e-book)

Stock or custom editions of BroadStreet Publishing titles may be purchased in bulk for educational, business, ministry, fundraising, or sales promotional use. For information, please email orders@ broadstreetpublishing.com.

Design by Garborg Design at GarborgDesign.com
Typeset by Katherine Lloyd at theDESKonline.com

Printed in the United States of America
20 21 22 23 24 5 4 3 2 1

Contents

Preface

Thousands upon thousands of books have been written about marriage. Hundreds upon hundreds of marriage retreats and seminars are offered every year. Teaching and instructions on how to have a better marriage are clearly in demand. But what are couples really desiring? What are they looking for in marriage books or retreats? What does a better marriage look like?

Most couples we know say they long for a more enriched relationship, a greater understanding of each other, better communication, a way to work more effectively through conflict, a more exciting and fulfilled sex life, a deeper emotional connection . . . the list goes on. Most marriage books and retreats attempt to offer these things, and many of us get help with our relationship for a season. But in a short time, so many of us are pretty much back to where we were before we started. What's the problem? Why is it so difficult to make positive lasting adjustments in our marriages?

Because change is hard. To make positive marital adjustments work and take hold requires a life change. And changed behavior doesn't come easily. We may even want to change for the good, but creating new pathways toward significant change really requires something significant of us. We need sufficient internal dissatisfaction (a sense we need a change), adequate external pressure (a reinforcement from others to change), and a positive model and blueprint for change (clearly seeing and under-standing what change looks like and what is required of us). When we have those three things, along with a true willingness to change, a rewarding and lasting trans-formation can take place. That is what happened in our marriages.

When I (David Ferguson) learned of Steve and Barbara Uhlmann's fascinating journey toward marital intimacy, it immediately struck me that they serve as an ideal model for transformational change. They were both "stuck" in a marital existence. At first, they didn't know how to change. But they eventually locked onto a life-change process that radically transformed their mere existence into an ongoing relational intimacy with each other.

And when I (Steve Uhlmann) learned of David and Teresa Ferguson's tried and proven blueprint for marital transformation, it struck me that they can provide couples the guidance toward the relational intimacy we all want and seek. Combining our forces has resulted in a step-by-step process of how you can respond to God's call to love your spouse as Jesus loves.

This is unlike any marriage book you have ever read. Mainly because it does more than give you words to read. This book offers specific biblical truths for you to experience which will change the way you think and act toward your spouse. Included in each chapter—following a series of daily devotionals—are experientials for you to engage in. These experientials will guide you to explore your own personal story, your marriage story, and Jesus' story—the One who has the power to bring change to your life. Don't skip over these exercises. They are what will bring about lasting change.

So don't think of this as a mere book. See it as your personal guided journey into marital intimacy. Along the way, you will discover that your relationship with your spouse is being positively changed—a change that can last a lifetime. It has for us, and it can for you. Let the journey begin.

David Ferguson
Steve Uhlmann

Introduction

WHY A 40-DAY JOURNEY?

Implementing any new discipline, creating a new habit, or learning a new skill requires practice. *Called 2 Love: A 40-Day Journey into Marriage Intimacy* is designed to guide you in the skills, habits, and experiences that cultivate lasting change—changes for more intimacy in your marriage!

The daily devotions will inspire you. The personal journal moments will encourage you to reflect on your personal story so you are ready to practice relational skills with your spouse. The "Marriage Staff Meetings" will guide your conversation with your partner and provide self-guided practice for true intimacy as you continue to build out your marriage story.

WHY DEVELOP YOUR OWN MARRIAGE STORY?

The personal and marriage journal moments are intended to support you as you develop your own marriage story. As you write your personal reflections, journal about the gratitude for your marriage, and chronicle the change God brings to your relationship, you will end up with a lasting record of the benefits of the Lord (Psalm 103:2). These remembrances will provide reassurance and hope when life brings challenges in the future. Clarifying your marriage story will also equip you to share it with others. You'll be prepared to share your story of hope as you share your hope in Jesus.

WHY ARE THERE MOMENTS WITH JESUS?
I THOUGHT THIS WAS A MARRIAGE BOOK

In this *Called 2 Love* resource, you will also practice moments of intimacy with Jesus. Intentional moments of time with him will increase your closeness with the One who is love. It will be these times of first experiencing God's love for you that will empower you to love your partner. It's only because of his love for us that we have hope of sharing that love with others. Jesus said it plainly: "You are to love each other. You must love each other as I have loved you" (John 13:34 NLV).

HOW TO USE THIS RESOURCE

Called 2 Love: A 40-Day Journey into Marriage Intimacy can be used in a variety of ways:

- **Devotional guide for couples:** This do-it-yourself guide can lead you and your spouse into greater closeness. Do the recommended exercises for maximum growth and intimacy!

- **Small group resource:** This journey into marriage intimacy can also be used in a 6-week format with a small group. When three to four couples share their experiences together, God has an amazing way of deepening impact.

- **Guide for marriage mentors and permarital counseling**: Marriage mentors will find this resource ideal for engaging couples who are struggling or just getting started in their marriage journey.

Called 2 Love: A 40-Day Journey into Marriage Intimacy is unique. It's unlike most marriage books because this resource is designed to give you regular doses of God's love for you and then encourages you to share that same love with your partner. You'll not only learn what an intimate marriage looks like, but you'll also learn the skills for *how* to make intimacy happen.

Each of the six weeks is structured the same.

- Days 1–4: Personal, daily devotionals with a story, short prayer, and reflections.

- Day 5: Journal about your personal story and reflect on your marriage story so the call to love becomes more personal.

- Day 6: Experience moments with Jesus through guided devotionals, and encounter his incredible love for you.

- Day 7: "Marriage Staff Meeting." Prepare your responses ahead of time and set aside one to two hours for deep and meaningful conversations with your spouse or small group.

GROW CLOSER TO YOUR SPOUSE,
GROW IN YOUR FAITH

Called 2 Love: A 40-Day Journey into Marriage Intimacy is not only designed to guide you into more closeness with your spouse, it is also designed to foster a Spirit-empowered faith—a faith that is demonstrable, observable, and only possible with the empowerment of the Holy Spirit.

A framework for this kind of spiritual growth has been drawn from a cluster analysis of several Greek and Hebrew words that declare that Christ's followers are to be equipped for works of ministry or service (See Ephesians 4:12).

Therefore, in this book you'll find specific notations around four themes (see Appendices 2–4) that help you become a Spirit-empowered disciple.

A SPIRIT-EMPOWERED DISCIPLE:

- **Loves the Lord**

  You will find specific exercises marked L1-10. These moments are specific times of expressing your love for Jesus.

- **Lives the Word**

  You will find certain exercises marked W1-10. These moments are designed to equip you in how to live out specific Scriptures from God's Word.

- **Loves People**

  You will find exercises marked P1-10. These moments help you discern the relational needs of others and sharing God's love in meaningful ways.

- **Lives His Mission**

  Finally, you will find specific exercises marked M1-10. These exercises are a part of actively sharing Jesus' life and telling others about the Jesus who lives inside of us.

Each Spirit-empowered outcome will be noted with the following symbol:

All forty Spirit-empowered Faith Outcomes are in Appendix 4 and are listed for your review.

Our world needs couples living as Spirit-empowered disciples who are making disciples who, in turn, make disciples. Thus, *Called 2 Love: A 40-Day Journey into Marriage Intimacy* rightly focuses on the powerful simplicity of:

- Receiving God's love for us and then loving him as our first priority.

- Living his Word, because there's power and possibility in experiencing Scripture.

- Loving people by developing a lifestyle of giving first, to your spouse and to others around you.

- Living his mission, which means building a lasting legacy as you share Jesus' hope with others.

DAY 1

Wake-Up Calls

For you have given him his heart's desire.

PSALM 21:2

God was thrilled for you on your wedding day. He loved seeing you celebrate with family and friends, and he loved being able to give you what your heart most desired—an intimate relationship with the man or woman of your dreams!

If you've been married any length of time, you've also experienced a few wake-up calls in your relationship. You have been reminded of the need to reprioritize and refocus on your marriage.

Your wake-up call may have included emotions that have grown cold or the realization of a growing distance between you and your spouse. Your wake-up call might have also included extreme conflict in your relationship, or perhaps you've found yourself or your spouse preoccupied with distractions outside your marriage. It is even possible one or both of you have threatened to leave the relationship.

When these wake-up calls happen, it is important for both husband and wife to learn what the other person *actually needs*.

The following story from the Ferguson's marriage helps illustrate what a wake-up call might sound like. As you read, see if you can identify with the challenges of keeping your own marriage a priority in the face of a busy life and competing priorities.

My Wake-Up Call

It had been another stressful yet fulfilling day of juggling a secular job and a demanding ministry to students. My (David) schedule had been packed with typical activities: an early morning discipleship group, a number of appointments at the office, lunch with a church elder, several phone calls from students, and another round of tinkering with a faulty computer program. I left a pile of work on my desk just in time to run home for a quick dinner. After dinner, I hurried off to the church for a counseling appointment and a committee meeting that lasted until ten.

By the time I got home that night, Teresa was in bed but still awake. I slipped into bed beside her and turned out the light. We talked in generalities about the day. I described my accomplishments, and she related how the kids had behaved—and misbehaved—at home.

At this point in our marriage, our conversations were rather superficial, as was the rest of our relationship. I was so busy with my job and leading a growing ministry, and she was so busy running the home that we rarely connected deeply with each other. We were not enemies, yet our marriage had a distance that was unsettling to me.

Staring up at the ceiling in the darkness, I addressed the issue. "Teresa, I sense a dryness between us, like we live on opposite sides of a big desert. We are so involved in our own separate worlds of activity that we hardly notice each other. Is this the way it's always going to be with us?"

There was silence on Teresa's side of the bed, followed by a deep sigh. "I don't know, David."

Finally I found the courage to ask the question that had been haunting me for months. "Teresa, do you really love me?"

Silence again. When Teresa finally answered, I was not prepared for the directness of her response. "David, I don't feel anything for you. I'm just numb."

That sobering exchange in our bedroom took place more than forty years ago. It was the beginning of an intense, sometimes painful, but ultimately fulfilling marital journey.

What was missing in our marriage was an ever deepening intimacy and it had something to do with what we genuinely *needed* from one another.

Pause and imagine what your marriage might need more of or less of.

"Speak Lord, your servant is listening"

1 SAMUEL 3:9

As you remember the various wake-up calls along your marriage journey, what is it that your partner, at the time, might have needed from you?

Say a prayer to the Lord. Tell him about your wake-up calls and how you want to learn. Write down what you hear as you listen to Jesus.

Lord, as I think back over our marriage, I realize my spouse has needed more _____ from me.

Help me to know and learn more about what my partner truly needs because . . .

♥ Claim the promise of John 13:34 — *"Love each other. Just as I have loved you."*

DAY 2

Clueless!

*Anyone who claims to know all the answers
doesn't really know very much.*

1 CORINTHIANS 8:2

I f we're really honest, at times, we are clueless about how to experience a truly intimate marriage. There are times when our spouse is a complete mystery to us.

Our only hope of loving our partner well is to acknowledge that what we claim to know is not sufficient! We need the Author of marriage to join us in this journey of marriage intimacy. We genuinely need the God, who is love, to show us and equip us in how to love our partner well.

Consider the following story from the Ferguson's journey. It reveals how the Lord is longing to join you in loving your spouse well.

Joining Jesus In Loving Well

Several years after Teresa's shocking disclosure that she felt emotionally numb in our relationship, a small but significant incident confirmed that something good was happening in our marriage. The distance between us was being gradually replaced by the oneness and intimacy we both craved.

Every year, Teresa and I try to get away just to focus on *us*. For many years, one of our favorite spots was a quiet, comfortable cabin in the Smoky Mountains. It became our own personal retreat, where the two of us could relax alone or with a few friends. One year, just before leaving home for the airport and our pilgrimage to Tennessee, I passed by the kitchen and sensed God prompting this new thought: *Why don't you take a few packets of Sweet 'N Low with you for Teresa?* Over the years of our marriage I had learned that Teresa prefers Sweet 'N Low over other sweeteners in her coffee, but the lodge where we usually stayed didn't serve that brand. So I reached into the kitchen cabinet for a handful of pink packets and slipped them into my briefcase.

We arrived at the cabin just in time for dinner. As dessert and coffee were served, Teresa began searching the table for the Sweet 'N Low, disappointed again that it wasn't there. But I had come to the table prepared. As I pulled a small, pink packet out of my pocket and handed it to her, the disappointment on Teresa's face was washed away by an endearing smile. Tears filled her eyes, and she hugged me. I relished the pleasure I was able to bring to my wife with such a simple act. I also sensed God's pleasure at what had happened. He seemed to say, "We did well together, David! I needed you to bring the packets up the mountain and share them with Teresa, but you needed me to prompt you to bring them!"

I am convinced I never would have thought to bring the Sweet 'N Low on my own. God was thinking of Teresa that day, and he wanted to involve me in the ministry of caring for my wife in this special way.

Pause and imagine that your spouse might genuinely need what's not completely obvious. The good news is that God knows and wants to show you!

PRAYER AND REFLECTION

Share your heart with the Author of marriage. Tell him the things you've come to know and what you need to know.

God, I'm grateful that I have come to know how important it is to my spouse that I
_____, but there are times
when I need you to show me _____.

Now would be a good time to pray a prayer like this:

Lord, I need you to empower my love for my spouse. Please give me your wisdom for
how to love _____ well, and I ask for your Spirit's power to make it possible.

♥ Claim the promise of Romans 5:5 — "[I have] this hope [and it] will not lead to disappointment. For [I] know how dearly God loves us, because he has given us the Holy Spirit to fill our hearts with his love."

DAY 3

The *Issue* Is Not the Only Issue!

*We know that God causes everything to work together for the good
of those who love God and are called according to his purpose.*

ROMANS 8:28

Stuff happens in life. That's a guarantee. Jesus even told us that we would experience trouble in this life (John 16:33). Life events, whether positive or painful, must always be viewed through the lens of God's desire to bring forth *good*. This means we can experience the goodness God wants for us and deepened intimacy with our partner, no matter what the challenge.

Experiencing difficult moments with your spouse, *can* actually draw you closer together. As your inadequacies are exposed and God's love is shared, sweetness of intimacy is the result. Trying to fix a problem you're facing together is not nearly as important as coming to know what your partner really needs. This was certainly the story for Steve and Barbara Uhlmann.

As you read the Uhlmman's story, see how fears, anxieties, and inadequacies were exposed and how that set the stage for exploring what their marriage really needed.

Needs Revealed

"This is Barbara," I gasped. "Come get me. I'm in real trouble."

My hands were trembling so much I could barely get my cellphone back into my purse. I was just a short distance from home, and I knew my husband Steve would come quickly.

It had been a beautiful day. Coming off an extended vacation, I was casually strolling through the grocery store picking up needed goods. Then in aisle nine without warning I started sweating. It wasn't just the perspiration of a summer day in Arizona, but the drenching sweat of a body in distress. In seconds, my clothes were soaked.

I started shaking violently and couldn't stop. My body kept trembling and sweating until I was exhausted.

•••

When I (Steve) got Barbara's call, I freaked out. I had never heard her like that before.

As I ran into the store, I saw Barbara sitting on a couch just inside the entrance, violently shaking and soaked, as though somebody had dumped a bucket of water on her. Something was seriously wrong.

Fortunately, the hospital was close. I made the five-minute drive in two minutes and pulled up to the emergency room entrance. In no time, Barbara was whisked away to have tests run, and I collapsed into a chair filled with worry about my wife's health.

There is no better definition of frustration for someone with my temperament than being forced to sit in the midst of a crisis where I couldn't do anything to fix the problem. In my business career, I prided myself in analyzing problems and coming up with fixes. But in Barbara's case, I didn't even know what the problem was. Could Barbara be having a heart attack? A stroke? Did she have an aneurysm? I had no idea. With nothing to do but sit and wait, I imagined the worst. My sense of powerlessness grew with each passing moment.

After two or three hours of tests, examinations, and my deep concern that I could lose Barbara, the doctor finally appeared. I braced myself for the worst.

"We think your wife has suffered a panic attack."

"What's a panic attack?" I asked, relieved it wasn't a heart attack, but still puzzled.

"A panic attack is a sudden episode of intense fear that triggers severe physical reactions, even though there is no real danger," the doctor said.

That didn't really help. "What causes that?" I wondered. Something must have triggered it. I could not wrap my mind around something so real being triggered by a lack of real danger. How could the frozen food section of the grocery store bring on such uncontrollable symptoms? What did Barbara have to be afraid of?

• • •

None of it made sense to me (Barbara) either. If anything, I should have been more relaxed and happier than ever. After all, we had just come back from the best vacation of our lives.

Ultimately, I was diagnosed with adrenal stress disorder, chronic fatigue syndrome, and PTSD (Post-Traumatic Stress Disorder). Even with the more specific diagnosis, I still couldn't understand how that could be. I had never been in the military. What kind of traumatic stress could I be reacting to? Where was all this coming from and what could I do about it? What were Steve and I needing to learn? How in the world were we going to get through this together?

Pause and imagine that underneath some of life's significant pain and personal struggles lay opportunities to deepen closeness.

PRAYER AND REFLECTION

Let all that I am praise the Lord;
may I never forget the good things he does for me.

PSALM 103:2

Reflect on some of your life's challenges and how they ultimately brought positive impact to your marriage. Perhaps, you've experienced a financial or health challenge, a difficult pregnancy, or death of a loved one. You could have gone through a career setback, a child's trauma, or a shattered dream, but through it all you were drawn closer together. Now share your grateful heart with Jesus, the Author of marriage.

Jesus, as I recall us going through the challenge of _____ *,*
I celebrate the good things you did for us. Our marriage grew stronger because we . . .

Ask the Lord to give you wisdom and deepened love as you walk through future challenges.

Jesus, no matter what challenges we may face, teach me how to love _____
well. I know I will especially need your help and wisdom in . . .

♥ Claim the promise of James 1:5 — "If you need wisdom, ask our generous God, and he will give it to you."

DAY 4

Who *Really* Likes Change?

But the Holy Spirit produces this kind of fruit in our lives:
love, joy, peace, patience, kindness, goodness, faithfulness,
gentleness, and self-control. There is no law against these things!

GALATIANS 5:22–23

It has been said that the only person who really likes change is a baby with a wet diaper! That's a light-hearted way to introduce a serious topic. Truthfully, ever-deepening intimacy in your marriage will require change.

Because we are human, we simply don't love well. We need the perfecting work of the Holy Spirit for us to live and love like Jesus. Only he can produce things like love, joy, peace, patience, kindness, and goodness in relationships. In other words, some of the change that might be needed in your marriage, could be needed in you!

Read on to see how the Uhlmanns experienced this perfecting change.

Perfecting Change

I (Steve) didn't know what to think. There is no question Barbara's health issue got my attention. That attention meant a lot to Barbara, but I have to admit the whole thing frustrated me because I didn't know how to fix it. Back then, I saw everything in simple, mechanistic terms. Find the cause of the problem, fix it, and move on. Because I couldn't fix this problem, I didn't know what else to feel.

I had a wife who was being plagued with panic attacks, for God only knows why. How was I to respond to all this? I was looking for a plan, some specific course of action that could help me get through this situation. I did love Barbara, and she loved me. I just wanted to move on with life.

At first glance, our marriage together looked great. We had everything we needed physically. We lived in a lovely home. We weren't struggling financially. By all appearances, we had a great life together. Our spiritual needs were certainly being met. We both knew Jesus personally and had chosen, many years back, to follow him. We said we loved each other on a regular basis, but something was still missing relationally. We learned that the key to finding this missing piece was somehow related to deeper needs—needs we didn't even realize we had.

That put us on a journey of relational discovery. I (Steve) discovered that the more patience and kindness I expressed towards Barbara didn't "fix" her health issues, but we grew closer! Slowly, we began to unlock who we were and how God designed us to experience an ever-deepening love that resulted in an ever-growing emotional connection with one another. Through the changes God brought about in both of us, we discovered a depth of relational intimacy that we never thought possible.

Pause and imagine just one change that might bring significant, deepened intimacy in your marriage.

That is what this forty-day journey into marriage intimacy is about. You may have a wonderful marriage right now, or you may wish things were better between you and your spouse. Either way, you and I were called to love with an ever-increasing love. We invite you on this *Called 2 Love* journey so you can enjoy the immersive experience of relational intimacy with your partner. For that to happen consistently, some things may have to change. Consider some of those changes now.

> *But the Holy Spirit produces this kind of fruit in our lives:*
> *love, joy, peace, patience, kindness, goodness, faithfulness, gentleness,*
> *and self-control. There is no law against these things!*
>
> GALATIANS 5:22–23

Consider the various facets of love from Galatians 5:22–23 and ask the Lord for a fresh, deepened ability to express his love to your spouse.

Lord, as you perfect and complete your love in me, I want to demonstrate more love in my marriage. I specifically want to show my spouse more _____ (joy, peace, patience, kindness, goodness, faithfulness, gentleness, self-control) because . . .

Jesus, change me, so that we can experience more of the deeply intimate marriage you intend for us.

♥ Claim the promise of 1 John 5:14–15 — "[I am] confident that He hears [me] whenever [I] ask for anything that pleases Him. And since [I] know He hears [me] when [I] make requests, [I] also know that He will give [me] what [I] ask for."

Married but Still Alone

I will praise you, Lord, with all my heart; I will tell of all the marvelous things you have done.

PSALM 9:1

Making It Personal

The fifth day of each week is designed for you to pause, reflect, and journal about your personal journey in God's call to love. You'll reflect on how that calling is lived out in your personal life and in your marriage. Day Five will be a time to reflect and write about your personal story and build your marriage story. Let's begin to make it personal now.

Like the Uhlmanns and the Fergusons, couples can live together, even enjoy an intimate sexual relationship, yet still struggle to feel closeness emotionally and relationally. Deepened relational connections don't happen overnight. They require a continuing journey.

Take a moment and remember some of your favorite wedding memories. Recall your wedding day, the photos, the guests, the vows, and the reception. Now remember some of the highlights of your honeymoon, the romance, the adventure, and the thrill of a new life together. Those newlywed years may have been just a short time ago or they may feel like an ancient memory. Whether you have shared months or many years with your spouse, consider this:

- You can share a wedding and a honeymoon together and still feel alone.

- You can share the same address, the same dinner table, and even the same bed and still feel disconnected.

- You can live together for decades, have children and even grandchildren, and still feel distant and isolated from your spouse.

INTIMACY IS GOD'S ANSWER TO ALONENESS

Aloneness gives way to intimacy in marriage when:

- You are deeply known by one another.

- You experience genuine care for one another.

- Each partner is focused on giving to the relational needs of the other.

We experience a deepened sense of intimacy with the Lord through our times of prayer, worship, and personal encounters with him. In a similar way, marriage intimacy will require deepened, relational connection.

NOW IT'S TIME TO JOURNAL A BIT OF YOUR STORY

We invite you to spend a few moments reflecting and writing about your own relationship journey. You'll spend time journaling about your Personal Story and then your Marriage Story. Let's start working on your story here.

My Personal Story

Can you think of a time when God seemed very close? Write about your experience here. (For example: When my mother died, God's comfort was very present. When I felt discouraged about financial pressures, God encouraged me with patience until I received a raise. When I felt rejected by friends at work, God's love was very real.)

I really sensed God was there for me when . . .

My Marriage Story

Reflect on past times of deep closeness in your marriage: maybe honeymoon moments, memorable experiences together, your children's birth, etc. Celebrate God's goodness for these special times of intimacy.

I especially remember how close I felt in my marriage when . . .

DAY 6

How Are You Doing, Adam?

My Jesus Story

The sixth day of each week is designed for you to reflect on Jesus' story and how he has lavished his love upon you. You'll be encouraged to read and consider his story and then invited to write about your personal encounter with Jesus in your Jesus story. Let's begin Day Six now.

Then the Lord God said,
"It is not good for the man to be alone.
I will make a helper who is just right for him."

GENESIS 2:18

God's original plan for marriage was perfect. He created marriage to be a place of consistent, deepened intimacy. God intended marriage to be a place where aloneness is to be removed. Let's go back to the very beginning and see what the Creator intended.

In the beginning, God created the heavens and the earth and declared that it was good. He created Adam—the first man—and placed him in this perfect setting.

It sure seemed to be perfect.

- Adam lived in a perfect world and had a perfect relationship with God.

- He possessed everything in the world.

- He had a great position and was in complete charge of everything in his world.

In the midst of all of this goodness in the Garden, God looked down on the situation and said, "It is not good . . . " (see Genesis 2:18). Doesn't that seem odd? This was paradise on earth! What could possibly be "not good"?

His Story

TURNING NOT GOOD INTO VERY GOOD!

The Creator, who is completely sovereign and able to create Adam in any way he desired, chose to create Adam to need both a relationship with God and another human. Therefore God looked down in the midst of all that goodness in paradise and declared that something was not good—Adam was alone.

- Apparently, Adam needed both an intimate relationship with God *and* another person.

- And then God, in his abundant grace, not only declared the problem, but he also solved it. Adam was alone and in need of human relationship, so God provided: "I will create for you a helper."

- The Creator provided a companion in the person of Eve, and Adam's aloneness was removed.

- With Eve's arrival, God turned "not good" into "very good" (Genesis 2:18; 1:31).

- God's first intended purpose for marriage was this: through this divinely created relationship called marriage, aloneness would be removed.

WHERE ARE YOU, ADAM?

Consider this: After Adam and Eve had disobeyed God (Genesis 3) and sin entered the world, God went looking for Adam in the Garden. God asked a simple question: "Where are you?" What was going on in the heart of God when he asked this question of Adam?

- Was God's intention to find Adam and ridicule, shame, or lecture him? *No.*

- Did God ask the question because he planned to give Adam the silent treatment and never speak to him again? *Of course not.*

- Or was God's heart and divine intention to ask the question that ultimately revealed his plan for redemption and restoration? *Read on!*

There were certainly consequences to Adam's disobedience, but the heart of God was filled with compassion and love. We know this because God's redemption plan is revealed throughout all of Scripture. He is always reaching out to humanity.

WHERE ARE YOU?

How we view God's heart toward us determines our pursuit of intimacy with him and ultimately our intimacy with others. Listen as he asks the same question of you: *Where are you?* And remember, God's intention isn't to harm you, criticize you, or never speak to you again. Who would want to pursue closeness with that kind of "god"? Instead, imagine this kind of God.

Imagine you're a parent of a small child. You're in a busy shopping mall during the holidays. Hundreds of people are crowding the aisles, hustling to get to the next store. Your preschooler is intrigued and distracted by everything in sight. Then it happens! You're focused on a conversation with the salesperson, you look around, and your child is gone. You panic. You retrace your steps. Over and over, you're thinking to yourself, *Where are you?*

Consider the emotions that would flood your heart. You may be irritated at your child's impulsiveness and scared about the dangers of being separated, but underneath all that is your heart of love. Your irritation is no match for the compassion you feel as you imagine your child alone and afraid. The question, *Where are you?* is motivated by love. Now imagine the relief you would feel after being reunited with your child; the joy you would feel when the relationship and security are restored.

This is the kind of God we have. This is God's true character and heart of love for us.

Though God never has and never will lose sight of us, at times, we might fail to see him and his true character. Reflect on your perspective of God, just in case you've seen him in another way. The real God is longing to love you and to relate with you. When we have this perspective of the real God, it prompts our love of him and empowers our love for others.

Let's reflect on a specific passage of Scripture that confirms God's heart for us: "Yet the Lord longs to be gracious to you; therefore he will rise up to show you compassion" (Isaiah 30:18 NIV).

Your Jesus Story

Pause quietly to meditate on the Lord. Use your imagination to picture Jesus sitting at the Father's right hand. You, at times, have been the lost child, anxious and uncertain. And now he sees you with joy and excitement. He rises from the throne of heaven with compassion in his heart to embrace you, to welcome you, and to love you. Take a moment and let your heart celebrate this kind of Jesus!

Jesus, when I imagine you arising from your throne to welcome me, I . . .

Now imagine him welcoming you with compassion: "Yet the Lord longs to be gracious to you; therefore he will rise up to show you compassion" (Isaiah 30:18 NIV).

Jesus, as I reflect on your compassion toward me, I . . .

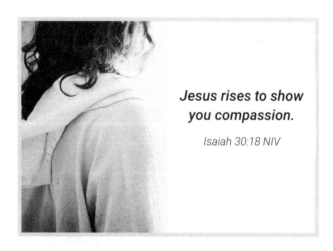

Jesus rises to show you compassion.

Isaiah 30:18 NIV

W1. A Spirit-empowered disciple falls in love with Jesus more and more because of spending consistent time in God's Word.

DAY 7

Sharing Your Week 1 Journey

May they experience such perfect unity that the world will know that you sent me and that you love them as much as you love me.

JOHN 17:23

Marriage Staff Meeting

The following exercises are to be completed on your own but then shared in a Marriage Staff Meeting. A Marriage Staff Meeting is a special time that is set aside just for you and your partner. You will need at least an hour of uninterrupted, scheduled time to talk. This will be the time to share your personal, marriage, and Jesus stories with your spouse. Let this time be an opportunity to open your heart to one another. Be sure to accept your partner's responses, offering no criticism or judgment. Simply share your stories together. After completing these exercises as a couple, you may also want to do the same with other couples in a small group setting.

In this Marriage Staff Meeting, you and your partner will focus on some of the key themes that can remove aloneness in your relationship. You'll connect with one another spiritually as you talk about your experience with Jesus and how he rises to show you compassion (Isaiah 30:18). You will connect with your partner emotionally and prioritize your marriage as you learn the critical skill of celebrating together. You'll want to look for opportunities each day to share these positive moments with your spouse and then rejoice together.

Complete the following exercises on your own first, then be ready to talk about them during your Marriage Staff Meeting. You are on your way to a more intimate marriage.

Share a Personal Story

Just like the *Called 2 Love* stories from the Uhlmanns and the Fergusons, we can all get distracted from our journey of marriage intimacy. There are times when each of us can be preoccupied with good things that keep us from the closeness we desire. What can preoccupy or distract you from marriage intimacy? Write your response below:

Sadly, at times I can be distracted from making our marriage a priority when I become preoccupied with . . . (my job, the kids, activities, hobbies, my family, etc.)

Share Your Marriage Stories

We love because He first loved us.

1 JOHN 4:19 NIV

God has created each of us to need both an intimate relationship with himself, through his Son, Jesus Christ, and we also need meaningful relationships with others—especially our spouse! God's intended purpose for marriage is that a husband and wife would enjoy such closeness and intimacy that neither partner would feel alone! Privately reflect on this priority:

- Husbands, perhaps this could be a new measure for a successful marriage. Does your wife feel less alone now than ever?

- Wives, does your husband feel less alone now than ever?

Share your response from page 20.

I especially remember how close I felt in our marriage when . . .

Then continue sharing these reflections with your partner.

🗨 *When I think about how God has called me to love my wife/husband, I . . .*

🗨 *As I think about how God wants so much closeness in our marriage that neither of us feels alone, I . . .*

Share Your Reflections from Your Jesus Stories

Pause quietly to remember your meditation with the Lord. You used your imagination to picture Jesus sitting at the Father's right hand. You, at times, have been the lost child, anxious and uncertain. Now he sees you with joy and excitement. He arises with compassion in his heart to embrace you, to welcome you, and to love you. Allow your heart to celebrate this kind of Jesus!

🗨 *As I reflect on Jesus' initiative to rise and show me compassion and grace, I . . .*

🗨 *As I consider that I have been called to love others like Jesus has loved me, I . . .*

 W1. A Spirit-empowered disciple falls in love with Jesus more and more because of spending consistent time in God's Word.

Doing the Bible

Rejoice with those who rejoice.

ROMANS 12:15A

Called 2 Love means truly knowing and being known. It means:

- **Knowing your spouse**—an intimate relationship involves a deep knowing of another person.

  This aspect of intimacy comes from the Hebrew word *yada*, which at times is translated "intimate" (see Jeremiah 1:5).

- **Disclosing to your spouse**—an intimate relationship involves vulnerable disclosure of who you are to another person.

  This aspect of intimacy comes from the Hebrew word *sod*, which at times is translated "intimate" (see Proverbs 3:32).

- **Caring involvement**—an intimate relationship involves a deep mutual knowing for the purpose of caring involvement.

  This aspect of intimacy comes from the Hebrew word *sakan*, which is sometimes translated "intimate" (see Psalm 139:3).

Complete this exercise as one way to experience all three of the Hebrew words that can be translated as "intimate"—knowing, disclosing, and caring involvement.

Think about a positive memory of your childhood (before age 12). Remember a pleasant memory—a time when you felt loved, cared for, special, appreciated, or affirmed. It might be your best birthday memory, favorite fishing trip, first bicycle, etc.

💬 *I remember when . . .*

Now share this positive memory with your partner. Your partner will celebrate and rejoice with you. Be sure to take turns so that you both share a positive memory and rejoice with each other.

How do I rejoice or celebrate with my spouse?

- It will involve expressing what you feel for your partner as you hear about his or her memory.

- Do you feel happy, glad, joyful, grateful, excited or pleased?

- That's what you share—the *emotions* you feel because your partner experienced this event!

Here's what rejoicing might sound like:

- *I'm so glad that happened!*

- *I'm thrilled you have that memory.*

- *I'm excited for you; that must have been terrific!*

Try this exercise now. Do Romans 12:15a by rejoicing with one another.

As a final step in the exercise, reflect on how God must have been blessed as he watched his children actually experiencing his truth! Close this time of sharing with prayer. Pray together and ask God to continue to deepen your call to love your husband/wife and to consistently do his Book.

• • •

As you experienced Romans 12:15a, you also disclosed something about yourself, deepening your intimacy, care, and knowing of one another. During this exercise, you may have even heard a memory you haven't heard before, and this helped you to better know your spouse. You experienced all three dimensions of intimacy, and you met your partner's need for what we call "attention"!

Plan to incorporate this practice of celebrating together on a daily basis. Celebrate over dinner each evening or before you go to sleep at night. Experience Romans 12:15a as you rejoice with those who rejoice. Celebrating regularly together draws us closer and guards us from being preoccupied with other things!

Be sure to experience this exercise again as a small group if you're going through this resource with other couples!

 W7. A Spirit-empowered disciple consistently looks for new ways God's Word can be lived out in life—looking for ways it can bring transformation in ongoing ways.

HERE'S A SUMMARY OF YOUR WEEK 1 JOURNEY

CALLED 2 LOVE MEANS:

- Aloneness is replaced by intimacy.

- Truly knowing and being known.

MARRIAGE INTIMACY IS DEEPENED AS YOU CONTINUE DOING THE BIBLE AND EXPERIENCING:

- Isaiah 30:18 — God's grace and compassion toward you!

- Romans 12:15a — Rejoicing with those who rejoice.

YOUR RELATIONSHIP WITH JESUS IS DEEPENED AS YOU:

- Imagine Jesus rising to show you grace and compassion.

- Imagine Jesus giving himself—just for you.

DAY 8

Priorities

Unless the Lord builds the house,
they labor in vain who build it.

PSALM 127:1 NASB

Reflect on your wedding day and what you dreamed would be your marriage priorities.

For most of us, our imagined priorities included something like this: "After my spouse's relationship with God, I anticipate being *first* priority. Children, friends, work, other family members, ministry, and hobbies come after me and our marriage."

Now, fast forward several years and ask yourself: "Have I possibly begun to take our marriage for granted? Have misplaced priorities set in, leaving us feeling alone at times?"

Read about the Ferguson's struggle with priorities. That struggle began *on their honeymoon!*

Honeymoon Hurts

Teresa and I were both sixteen years old and still in high school when we got married. Neither of us was a Jesus follower at the time. The whirlwind romance began with our first date. We went out for a soda, and then I took Teresa to the county jail to visit a crazy buddy of mine. Looking back, it wasn't the smartest way to begin a relationship!

Despite a less-than-romantic beginning, Teresa and I fell in love. Six months later, we faced our parents with a rebellious ultimatum: "We have decided to get married. If you don't give your permission, we will elope to Kansas where marriage at our age is legal." Our parents shed tears at our wedding, but they were not tears of joy.

Teresa and I spent our wedding night in a local motel. Early the next morning while Teresa was still asleep, a friend of mine knocked on the door of our room. Stanley and I were pool-shooting buddies, and he wanted me to go shoot pool with him. The fact that I was on my honeymoon didn't seem to matter to Stanley, and it didn't make much difference to me. I loved playing pool, so I got dressed, and we left. It never entered my mind to tell Teresa, who was still asleep. I simply walked out the door.

Teresa tells what happened next: "When I woke up and found David and his car gone, I didn't know what to think. Had I displeased him already? Had he changed his mind about being married to me? I felt confused and abandoned. So I left the motel and walked the several blocks home to my parents, crying and feeling very alone."

Somehow Teresa and I survived that rocky beginning. Yet I had communicated through my behavior that she was not the most important priority in my life. Without the tools to deal with such deep insensitivity and selfishness on my part, Teresa buried her pain, and we simply carried on with life. That honeymoon experience was in effect the first layer of hurt. It would grow to become a truckload of unresolved hurt over the next fifteen years.

Obviously, God wanted much more for us in our marriage than what we experienced those early years. He wanted our relationship to remove the aloneness we both felt. He wanted us to experience the oneness for which he created us and for which we both longed. God had something in mind, and he graciously began to let us in on his plan.

 Pause and imagine your marriage experiencing an ever-deepening intimacy that drives out the pain of aloneness.

They shall become one flesh.

GENESIS 2:24 NASB

This passage of Scripture reminds us how we can begin to prioritize or reprioritize the intimacy in our marriage. After your relationship with God, do you and your partner share a oneness of perspective and experience about the priorities in your marriage?

What would your spouse say are your top priorities? What is your spouse *experiencing* as your top five life priorities?

- _____
- _____
- _____
- _____
- _____

Where would God, work, friends, children, family members, and hobbies fit on this list?

Remember, what you *say* are your top priorities may be different than what is experienced or perceived by your spouse.

The hope of marriage intimacy, or "two becoming one," involves an honest and vulnerable journey in making your spouse a *true priority*.

Next, we invite you to reflect on your marriage relationship and the gratitude you feel. Taking the time to be grateful for your spouse and your marriage grows your joy and happiness. That's helpful for you personally and for your relationship. Let this exercise be a part of reprioritizing your spouse and your marriage. Take a few moments and write about your marriage!

As you do this exercise, you will bring joy to the heart of God. He will smile because you will actually be doing the Bible. You're not just reading the Bible. You'll be living it out. God loves it when we do his Word!

Write at least three reasons you are grateful for your spouse. Give thanks for your relationship. As you write, you'll be doing Ephesians 1:16, "I do not cease giving thanks for you, while making mention of you in my prayers" (NASB).

I'm grateful for my spouse and our marriage today for at least three reasons:

1. _____

2. _____

3. _____

♥ Claim the promise of Galatians 5:13 as you make your spouse your significant priority: "Through love serve one another."

L1. A Spirit-empowered disciple makes a consistent practice of thanksgiving and gratitude for all things and in all circumstances.

DAY 9

Know Me . . .
and Still Love Me

When Jesus came to the place, He looked up and said to him,
"Zacchaeus, hurry and come down, for today I must stay at your house."

LUKE 19:5 NASB

Marriage brings a depth of knowing each other that, at times, is intense and challenging.

It is important in our *Called 2 Love* journey to routinely experience the "Zacchaeus Principle." In this principle, we remember the accepting love that Jesus had for a tax collector and how we are called to love the same.

Each of us, as imperfect humans, have some rough edges which can irritate our partner. These rough edges create anything but intimacy! So how do we respond? Do we react with our own imperfections, or do we relate with God's unconditional love?

Read about David's memorable journey with his grandfather. This story gives an important insight into loving like Jesus and how we express his love for others.

An Example of Unconditional Love

At the age of sixteen, I (David) was already married and had graduated early from high school. I had two jobs and was a full-time student at a local community college. Even with all my adult responsibilities, I still had a lot of growing up to do. My grandfather was a key person who pointed me in the right direction. Here's an example. Between our home in Texas and the community college I attended lay about thirty miles of open highway. But I had a problem. The highway patrol often monitored this stretch of road, so I was getting pulled over for speeding every month or two. It soon got to the point that I was about to lose my license if I were stopped for speeding one more time.

Granddad was very wise and lived what I would later come to understand as a Spirit-empowered faith. I liked him a lot. One Sunday afternoon, he pulled me aside for a man-to-man chat about my speeding. As I surveyed Granddad's face, I sensed he had a plan.

"You got an idea, Granddad?" I asked.

"Sure do," he replied. "I'll loan you my truck, and the police will never know it's you."

I was sure I had found a kindred spirit. Granddad seemed to understand me. I eagerly agreed to his plan, and we walked to the shed to get Granddad's truck.

The next morning I made my way toward the highway, excited about pulling one over on the law. As I turned onto the open road, I roared through the gears to get the old truck up to my customary speed. But when I reached 55 mph, the speedometer stopped moving. Even though my foot pressed the accelerator to the floorboard, the truck would go no faster.

I was puzzled for a moment, then a smile broke over my face. Pretty soon I was laughing out loud. My wise grandfather had put one over on me! He knew the whole time that his truck wouldn't go faster than 55 mph. I drove Granddad's truck for the rest of the term and didn't get any more citations. More importantly, the incident deepened my relationship with my grandfather. He became a powerful influence in my life for good.

What was it about Granddad that prompted change in my life where others had failed? Cajoling and hounding from my wife and parents had only encouraged the rebel in me. The law's threat to revoke my license had not slowed me down. What had Granddad provided that the others had not?

Granddad modeled for me my own experience of Christ's accepting, welcoming love—just like Zacchaeus! When I became a Jesus follower, I realized that the Holy Spirit had used my granddad's acceptance to help me see God for who he really was.

Pause and imagine the joy of being deeply known and cared for by someone who loves you.

Or do you think lightly of the riches of His kindness and tolerance and patience,
not knowing that the kindness of God leads you to repentance?

ROMANS 2:4 NASB

When complaints, criticism, and cajoling haven't produced the desired changes in another person, rely on the kindness of the Lord!

We learn from the Zacchaeus story that accepting the love of Jesus was the key to their relationship *and* the changed behavior. Jesus looked beyond Zacchaeus' faults and saw his needs. Zacchaeus was touched with gladness because of Jesus' acceptance. During dinner, he was transformed by the kindness of the Lord (Luke 19:5–10). This same insight will serve every couple and every family well.

Both you and your spouse have some rough edges; you each have imperfections. As these rough edges are refined, conflicts will decrease, and intimacy will deepen. *How you pursue this transforming work is critical to success. You and your partner* need to change in certain ways, but *who* is the best change agent, you or the Holy Spirit? Allow Jesus to do the changing; you prioritize the loving. Talk about this with Jesus now.

Lord, move me from reacting, to responding with your love. Help me look beyond my partner's imperfections and see their needs. I specifically need your help as I . . .

Pause and reflect on typical complaints and rough spots in your marriage, then consider what the kindness of the Lord might look like as it is lived out through you.

Accept each other just as Christ has accepted you.

ROMANS 15:7

♥ Claim the promise of Romans 15:7 as you look beyond your partner's faults and meet his or her needs.

DAY 10

Life Happens

Now to Him who is able to do far more abundantly beyond all that we ask or think, according to the power that works within us, to Him be the glory in the church and in Christ Jesus to all generations forever and ever. Amen.

EPHESIANS 3:20–21 NASB

For marriage to be far more abundant and beyond what we can ask or think, we must intentionally focus on marriage *intimacy* as our goal. This is essential. Too often, we may find that . . .

- Our intimacy is hindered by unresolved relationship issues or emotions that have nothing to do with our marriage or spouse.

- We are distracted from God's best for our marriage by seemingly good things like work, friends, children's activities, hobbies, and even religious pursuits.

Before reading this next story from the Uhlmann's journey, pause and pray something like: *God, reveal any of my unhealed emotions and how they might be hindering intimacy with my partner. Show me any distractions that can leave my partner feeling alone.*

Together but Not Connected

"Goodbye, honey," my dad said as he raised his hand, waving it slightly. "Goodbye, and I'm so sorry."

I (Barbara) remember at the age of nine, sitting in the back seat crying as my mother drove away from my dad. I loved my dad very much, and I didn't understand why he left us. I couldn't figure out why my parents had to divorce. The only thing I concluded was that my own dad didn't love me enough to want to be with me. That wasn't true, of course, but that's what my young mind reasoned. It hurt so much. Emotionally, I felt the pain of abandonment.

I did my best to stifle my sobs and bury my hurt. That's what our family did. My sister, brother, and I were expected to stuff our feelings. We were never allowed to talk about why my dad left or how we felt about it. If you displayed any negative emotions such as anger or frustration with things not going your way, you were forced to go to your room until you got them under control. This seemed to contribute to me fearing a lot of things, both as a child and even in my marriage.

••••

As a young bride, I dreamed of sharing my life with Steve and enjoying the happiness of being with the man I loved. However, I didn't really understand what allowed love to deepen and grow, especially when we hit some rough patches.

At the beginning of our marriage, the euphoria of romantic love seemed to override the emotional baggage of my childhood pain, at least through the honeymoon. For me, the honeymoon ended sooner than I had hoped. What happened? Simply put, life happened. As with every marriage, we experienced a conflict here, a trouble-spot there, and a crisis every once in a while.

Two months after we were married, Steve set out to start a business. I was working as a teller at Valley National Bank, and my job kept a roof over our heads and food on the table. Steve spent long days trying to make the business go and often dragged home late for supper.

I was sitting in our living room reading a book when I heard the door open.

"I'm home," Steve called out as he let the door slam behind him. "What's there to eat?"

"It's in the refrigerator," came my flat reply. I didn't bother to get up.

Steve made his way into the living room. It was past 9:00 p.m.

"I made a chicken dinner," I stated, not looking up from my book. "I waited until seven and then just ate alone—like I did last night and the night before."

"Oh, that's okay," Steve said waving his hand toward me. "I had chicken for a late lunch. I'll just get some cold cereal. You wanna come in the kitchen while I eat? I can tell you how my day went."

I slowly made my way to the kitchen to join my husband.

"Steve," I questioned, "why can't you just call me when you're going to be late like this?"

"Oh, I'm sorry," came the reply. "The day just got away from me, but boy are things beginning to take shape."

•••

I (Steve) would like to say that the above scene just took place once or twice, but it didn't. This became a pattern. I was preoccupied with my work. Barbara would come home from her teller's job, eat alone, and then read a book. I would come home late all excited about my work and wanting Barbara to get excited with me.

It wasn't that she didn't care about the business I was trying to build. She was just hoping I would focus a little bit on building a marriage relationship with her. I wanted to give her things, while she just wanted me.

•••

I (Barbara) voiced very little of my concern about Steve's workaholic tendencies. Instead of opening up and letting Steve know how I felt, I kept clammed up. Instead of blowing up, I gave up. Instead of holding on to the dream of a deepened relationship, I let go of it.

Steve and I were together but not really connected. We were married to each other, yet we both felt emotionally alone.

Pause and imagine how your spouse may, at times, experience aloneness in your marriage.

O Lord, You have searched me and known me. You know when I sit down and when I rise up; You understand my thought from afar. You scrutinize my path and my lying down, And are intimately acquainted with all my ways.

PSALM 139:1–3 NASB

How might your spouse, at times, actually experience aloneness in your marriage?

My spouse may be feeling alone at times when I . . .

In contrast to an abundant and intimate marriage is a marriage that settles for less than God intends. We can be committed but not really connected. We can be a couple who is making a living but not really sharing a life. We can be together but too often still alone.

Pause and ask the Lord to be the Great Physician for you and your spouse. He can heal both unresolved pain and any misplaced priorities that hinder your freedom to love.

Father, I'm asking you to be the Great Physician for me and _____. Heal our hurt from the past. Be the God of all comfort who heals unresolved pain and the Spirit of power who reorders the priorities of our lives. I'm asking specifically for you to . . .

♥ Claim the promise of 1 Chronicles 29:11 for the Lord to have dominion over your marriage: "Yours, O Lord, is the greatness and the power and the glory and the victory and the majesty, indeed everything that is in the heavens and the earth; Yours is the dominion, O Lord, and You exalt Yourself as head over all" (NASB).

DAY 11

You Are Loved!

*And He said to him, "'You shall love the Lord your God with all
your heart, and with all your soul, and with all your mind.'
This is the great and foremost commandment. The second is like it,
'You shall love your neighbor as yourself.'"*

MATTHEW 22:37–39 NASB

Loving God and loving our neighbor are the greatest priorities of life. If you're married, your closest neighbor is your spouse. This truth certainly defines a foremost priority as a husband or wife.

Here's another important connection: loving your spouse as your neighbor or "near one" is grounded in loving yourself. Only when we embrace our worth to God are we free to love our partner like we have been loved by Jesus.

Your worth has been determined through the gift of Jesus at Calvary. Nothing that you do or don't do can distract from his declaration of your worth to him.

When we're in the midst of life's challenges and traumas, we often seem to question God's love for us the most. The more we experience Jesus' reassurance of our worth to him and his love for us, the more we find freedom to love others. Read about the Uhlmann's story next and then reflect on your worthiness to the Lord.

You Are Worth His Love

Soon after my first panic attack, Steve made sure I (Barbara) had someone to help me with the physical demands of the house and my health. To help me through emotionally, we called on a family friend who was a certified life coach. Linda came to our house almost daily to walk me through a recovery process. She is the one who encourage me to begin journaling.

Linda helped me realize that all my people pleasing efforts and all my doing was an attempt to prove that I was acceptable and worth loving. I wanted people, especially Steve, to care about being with the real me, but deep within I didn't feel worthy of it. This was embedded in a little girl so many years ago when her daddy abandoned her. Her emotions concluded that her daddy, the most important person in her life at the time, didn't consider her valuable enough to stay with her. He wanted instead to leave her. That wasn't really true, of course, but that is what became an emotional reality for me as a little girl.

Every summer, my siblings and I were allowed to spend a short time with my dad. Once we went back home, we could not speak of him and heard nothing from him until the next year. We did receive birthday and Christmas gifts, but no letters. When we sent my dad gifts, he sent them back with an explanation, "I can't accept any gifts from you because your mother probably paid for them."

That rejection deeply hurt. It fueled my sense of abandonment until it festered into a deep sense of unworthiness that was alive and well in the emotions of a grown up Barbara. Linda led me to deal with my lack of self-worth. Mainly, because it was keeping me from receiving a renewed love from Steve. It was also keeping me from seeing myself as a valued child of God, created in his image. That was keeping me from unselfishly loving myself so I could love Steve as God intended.

I desperately wanted to learn how to deal with all this. I became "still" before God, talked to him through my journal, and then listened for what he wanted to teach me.

On October 30th, I wrote in my journal:

> *God had to put me flat on my back to get my attention. He wants me to stop "doing"—running on the treadmill—and start "being." I am in the process of integrating my emotional self with my rational self. What an exciting journey!*

This journal entry, and many more, chronicled my experiences of love from God, love for myself, and then love *for* Steve.

Pause and visualize how rich your marriage will be as you learn how to experience more of God's love for you.

But God demonstrates His own love toward us,
in that while we were yet sinners, Christ died for us.

ROMANS 5:8 NASB

Consider some of the same penetrating questions related to your worth and value to the Lord.

Think about this question first: *What have you done this week to prompt the Lord to love you more?*

Before you respond—the answer is NOTHING! Remember that God has already demonstrated his great love for you, in that while you were still a sinner, he sent his Son to die for you. Your worth has been declared. You are worth the gift of Jesus!

Scripture also reminds us that, "He saved us, not on the basis of deeds which we have done in righteousness, but according to His mercy, by the washing of regeneration and renewing by the Holy Spirit" (Titus 3:5 NASB).

Pause to reflect on the truth that Jesus gave his life just for you! Not only for the whole world, but also for you! That is your identity. *You are the beloved of God.* Talk to God and let him know how this makes you feel.

Thank you, Father, that my worth has been securely established by your gift of Jesus.
I'm amazed and grateful that I am the "beloved of God" because . . .

♥ Claim the promise from John 13:34 that you are the "beloved" of God: "A new commandment I give to you, that you love one another, even as I have loved you, that you also love one another" (NASB).

DAY 12

Unlocking the Mystery of Relational Needs

And my God will supply all your needs according to His riches in glory in Christ Jesus.

PHILIPPIANS 4:19 NASB

Making it Personal

The promise of marriage intimacy is found in something deeper than endless activity, successful career, or plenty of possessions and money. God's promise of intimacy *is* attainable when we courageously explore the truth that the real needs in our lives and in our marriages may be deeper than we initially thought.

To begin making this personal, let's take a courageous look at how we were created to relate. We know our basic, physical needs remain constant throughout our lives; human beings never reach a developmental stage where food, water, sleep, or oxygen become optional. It is important that we recognize that the same consistency holds true for our relational needs. We need intimate, close relationships whether we're eight months or eighty years old.

Here's one way to emphasize this truth. Relational needs are generally easy to see in children. Even if they are comfortable, fed, and well-rested, infants may cry just because they want *attention*. Similarly, toddlers who fall down may cry even though they are not badly hurt. They have a need for *comfort*. Some children have a hard time separating from mom or dad, signaling their desire for *affection* or need for *security*. Other kids may try to get their parents to notice their academic, artistic, or athletic abilities because of their human need for *approval* or *appreciation*.

In contrast, the relational needs of adults are sometimes less visible. This does not mean however, that we gradually grow out of our relational needs or that our needs can somehow be met once and for all. Rather, it is merely an indication that as adults, we often try very hard to conceal or deny our relational needs we so freely expressed as children.

We are hardwired to need relationships. It may be painful for us to admit, but it's true. We were created by a sovereign God with certain physical, spiritual, and relational needs. Our condition of neediness requires that we look beyond ourselves and learn to care and trust in important relationships. We also cannot meet our relational needs alone. We cannot manufacture by ourselves the intangible value we realize when other people connect with us emotionally, know us intimately, and care for us in meaningful ways.

NEEDY BY DESIGN

All people have needs. In fact, as humans, we have needs in every dimension of our being:

- **Physical needs** – These are obvious to us—air, food, water, and sleep.

- **Spiritual needs** – We need peace, faith, forgiveness, and purpose in our lives.

- **Relational needs** – Just as real as physical needs but not as apparent, these are needs that can only be met through meaningful relationships with others.

A more thorough description of these needs will be addressed later in this resource, but here is an initial list of ten selected relational needs.

- Acceptance
- Affection
- Appreciation
- Approval
- Attention
- Comfort
- Encouragement
- Respect
- Security
- Support

Think about your needs in this way:

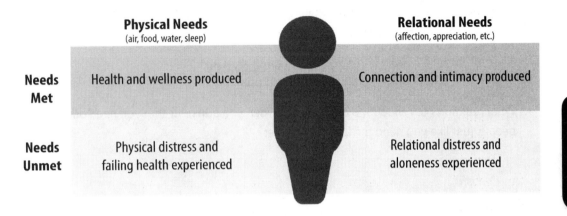

	Physical Needs (air, food, water, sleep)	**Relational Needs** (affection, appreciation, etc.)
Needs Met	Health and wellness produced	Connection and intimacy produced
Needs Unmet	Physical distress and failing health experienced	Relational distress and aloneness experienced

Another way to summarize the impact of these needs in our relationships is:

Relational Needs UNMET = Bad Things Happen
Relational Needs MET = Good Things Happen

Here's what this formula looks like in the Ferguson's and the Uhlmann's stories. For Teresa, when her needs for attention and affection went UNMET, love grew cold and her emotions grew numb. Bad things happened in her and David's marriage.

With David's thoughtfulness and caring initiatives, love returned to their marriage. Good things happened when relational needs were MET!

For Barbara, it went something like this: When needs for security and attention were UNMET, bad things happened like panic attacks, physical symptoms, emotional withdrawal, and distraction with things to do.

In contrast, when her needs for security and attention were MET by Steve, good things resulted. She felt more loved, peaceful, and motivated. Barbara came to experience fewer physical problems and ultimately no panic attacks.

David's and Steve's relational needs were not as immediately obvious to them, but they, too, came to understand the different results of relational needs being met or unmet. As David and Steve continue to tell their stories, you'll read about their own needs for affection, security, approval, encouragement, and support.

My Personal Story

What reactions or reflections do you have when you consider that *you need other people*, just like you need air, food, and water?

What thoughts and reflections come to mind when you also consider that *other people need you*?

Learning to meet and give to your partner's relational needs is vital to a healthy, thriving marriage. Look again on the next page at the ten relational needs with their definitions. Check (✓) the three needs you consider most important in your relationship with your spouse.* Which of these do you need most right now?

My Marriage Story

Here are the ten most common relational needs and the scriptural references for them. Understanding these relational needs will help you and your spouse increase your focus on giving to one another. Giving to one another in these ways is the key to relational closeness!

Check (✓) three of the Ten Relational Needs you consider most important in your relationship with your spouse.*

	Acceptance: Receiving others willingly and unconditionally (even when their behavior has been imperfect) and loving them in spite of any differences that may exist between you (Romans 15:7).
	Affection: Expressing care and closeness through physical touch and through words such as "I love you" or "I care about you" (Romans 16:16; Mark 10:16).
	Appreciation: Expressing thanks, praise, or commendation, particularly in recognition of someone's accomplishments or efforts (1 Corinthians 11:2).
	Approval (Blessing): Building up or affirming another person, particularly for who they are (as opposed to what they do); affirming both the fact and the importance of our relationship with another person (Ephesians 4:29).
	Attention: Conveying appropriate interest, concern, and care; taking notice of others and making an effort to enter into their respective worlds (1 Corinthians 12:25).
	Comfort: Caringly responding to a hurting person through words, actions, emotional responses, and physical touch; hurting with and for others in the midst of their grief or pain (Romans 12:15; Matthew 5:4; 2 Corinthians 1:3, 4).
	Encouragement: Urging others to persist and persevere in their efforts to attain their goals; stimulating others toward love and good deeds (1 Thessalonians 5:11; Hebrews 10:24).
	Respect: Valuing one another highly, treating one another as important, and honoring one another with our words and actions (Romans 12:10; 1 Peter 2:17).
	Security (Peace): Establishing and maintaining harmony in our relationships and providing freedom from fear or threat of harm through expressions of vulnerability, deepening of trust, and the successful resolution of conflict (Romans 12:16, 18).
	Support: Coming alongside others and providing gentle, appropriate assistance with a problem or struggle (Galatians 6:2).

---

* If you'd like a more objective assessment of your top three relational needs, we can help with that too. Go to greatcommandment.net/relationalneeds and take the Relational Needs Assessment.

Today, I think my top three relational needs might be:

1. _____

2. _____

3. _____

WEEK TWO

Now think for a moment about how your spouse has given to you and met one of these relational needs. Reflect on a recent example or a remembrance from the past and then express your gratitude.

Today, I'm grateful that my spouse met my need for _____ when . . .

♥ Claim the promise of Matthew 10:8 — "Give as freely as you have received!" And then express your gratitude to God for receiving.

DAY 13

Experience
Our Need-Meeting God

My Jesus Story

Give as freely as you have received!

MATTHEW 10:8

I t is important to recognize that we are needy, but it is equally important that we realize that God knows and cares about our needs. When we humbly express our needs and exercise faith, we experience God's love toward us, and he reassures us of his intent to provide. As God freely gives to us at the point of our need, we find freedom to gratefully give to others (Matthew 10:8).

The connection between human need, trusting faith, and divine provision is evident in many of the gospel stories—including Christ's ministry of acceptance for Zacchaeus.

His Story

THE POINT OF NEED

When Jesus came by, he looked up at Zacchaeus and called him by name. "Zacchaeus!" he said. "Quick, come down! I must be a guest in your home today." Zacchaeus quickly climbed down and took Jesus to his house in great excitement and joy.

(LUKE 19:5–6)

Zacchaeus was a tax collector. Being a tax collector in the first century meant he was under the authority of the Roman Empire. Because of Rome's influence, he was likely a thief and a traitor to his own people. The Gospel of Luke tells us that Zacchaeus was also short in stature, so out of what must have been loneliness, curiosity, and just pure necessity, the tax collector climbed a tree one day to get a good look at the Messiah. Zacchaeus had to question if Jesus would even notice him. He must have wondered if the Savior would reject him because of his actions (see Luke 19:1–27).

What a miracle Christ's invitation must have been to this tax collector! The Savior noticed him. He then asked Zacchaeus to share a meal, inviting him into one of the most intimate social settings of the day. This simple invitation was a deliberate offer of welcome, reception, and loving relationship. Jesus looked beyond Zacchaeus' faults and imperfections and saw his need.

In the midst of Zacchaeus' failures, Jesus offered compassion, companionship, and acceptance. It's also interesting to note what Jesus *didn't* do that day:

- Jesus didn't attack the tax collector's behavior, point out things that were wrong, or even give helpful advice.

- Jesus didn't remind Zacchaeus of what he *should* be doing or criticize him for not taking more responsibility.

- Jesus didn't give a religious lecture or make comparisons with other tax collectors in town.

- Jesus didn't try to manipulate change in Zacchaeus or withhold affection from him.

The Savior simply looked beyond Zacchaeus' flaws and mistakes and met him at the point of his need—the need of acceptance.

Your Jesus Story

Jesus offers this same invitation to you today. Jesus notices you. Just like he noticed Zacchaeus, the Savior notices you and your marriage. He's not too busy, and he's not too preoccupied to see your need.

Jesus sees you and offers an invitation of welcome, reception, and loving relationship. And just as miraculously, the Savior looks beyond your flaws and mistakes and wants to meet your needs.

Write a response. Tell God what it does to your heart to imagine Jesus noticing you, welcoming you, accepting you, and inviting you into relationship with him.

God, when I imagine this kind of love for me, I . . .

Jesus is welcoming you.

Luke 19:1–10

 L3. A Spirit-empowered disciple develops a correct view of God as the Lord reveals himself, enjoying more and more closeness with him.

DAY 14

Sharing Your Week 2 Journey

Serve one another in love.

GALATIANS 5:13

Marriage Staff Meeting

As you have your Marriage Staff Meeting this week, use the following exercises to guide your conversation. Take your time. Keep the focus positive and upbeat. Make this a time to know your spouse more deeply. Prioritize your own vulnerability. Stay away from blame or finger-pointing.

During these moments, you will want to love your partner like Jesus has loved you. Give only compassionate, accepting, and reassuring responses to your spouse.

If it's appropriate to address needs that are not being met in your relationship, give gracious responses. These responses might sound like:

- *I love you, and I'm looking forward to learning how to love you more.*

- *I'm sad that you don't experience me meeting your needs at times. I want to understand how important they are to you. I'm committed to loving you better.*

- *I'm glad we're having this conversation because I want to know how to love you in ways that are meaningful to you.*

Share Your Personal Story

💬 *Some of my top needs may be:*

Here again is the list of the ten most common relational needs. Take a moment to reflect on the three relational needs you listed on page 50 as most important to you. You may also want to refer to the Relational Needs Assessment in Appendix 1. Then reflect on and share how those needs impact you.

1. _____

2. _____

3. _____

RELATIONAL NEEDS

• Acceptance	• Comfort
• Affection	• Encouragement
• Appreciation	• Respect
• Approval	• Security
• Attention	• Support

💬 *When my needs are MET, good things happen like . . .* (for example: *I feel loved; I'm more patient; I have fewer physical complaints; I have fewer migraines; I am more open to sex; I'm more motivated to work on our relationship; etc.*)

💬 *When my relational needs go UNMET, sometimes bad things can happen like . . .* (for example: *I lash out in anger; I withdraw; I can't sleep; I get anxious; I feel resentful; I escape into my phone; I demand my way; etc.*)

Share Your Marriage Story

Share first with your spouse and then with your small group, if desired.

🗨 *I'm grateful for you. I'm especially thankful for the time you met my need for*
_____ when . . .

I have not stopped thanking God for you. I pray for you constantly.

EPHESIANS 1:16

Doing the Bible

Once you've chosen three of the relational needs previously mentioned, spend some time identifying how you would most like your spouse to meet those needs. Be specific. Read the examples below for ideas. As you share your needs and how you'd like your spouse to meet them, you'll be doing the Bible. You'll be living out Ephesians 4:15. You will be "speaking the truth in love."

My Needs	*How My Spouse Might Meet Them*
Acceptance	*Allow me to make mistakes—without criticism.*
Affection	*Hold and kiss me before you leave in the morning.*
Appreciation	*Affirm the effort I make to fix things at home.*
Approval	*Call unexpectedly just to tell me why you love me.*
Attention	*Talk for a few minutes each evening.*
Comfort	*Hold me and let me cry; gently reassure me that you care.*
Encouragement	*Pray with me when I'm struggling.*
Respect	*Ask my opinion about things to do for date night.*
Security	*Reassure me that I will be safe and taken care of.*
Support	*Pitch in to help with the kids, especially at bed time.*

Our partner shouldn't have to read our minds about how to meet our needs, so take the next few minutes to write down at least one of your top needs and how your partner can meet it.

💬 *One of my top relational needs is _____.*

💬 *I think this need for _____ is important to me because I feel loved in our marriage when _____.*

Repeat this exercise for each of your top 3 needs. Share your responses with your spouse. Be open. Be positive. Be vulnerable.

> *"Freely you received, freely give."*
>
> MATTHEW 10:8 NASB

Just as Christ freely gives you his acceptance and compassion, you are also called to give! Now that you have more clarity about one of your spouse's relational needs, plan to be more intentional in giving this week. Give to your spouse according to the needs they have shared.

💬 **Say these sentences to your spouse:**

As a part of living out my call to love, I'm looking forward to being more intentional about meeting your need for _____ by:

_____

_____

_____

_____

(For example, **attention** – *by doing more of the hobbies you enjoy;* **appreciation** – *by looking for ways to thank you and notice your effort around the house;* **support** – *by asking how I can help out or pitch in;* **respect** – *by asking for your ideas and input on things with the kids*)

 P3. A Spirit-empowerd disciple consistently discerns the relational needs of others and shares God's love in meaningful ways.

Imagine Jesus accepting you as you remember his invitation to Zacchaeus in Luke 19:5!

Share Your Reflections from Your Jesus Story

Remember your moments of meditation. Remember how Jesus notices you, accepts you, and invites you into relationship just as he did with Zacchaeus. Scripture tells us that Jesus is the same today as he was 2000 years ago. Hebrews 13:8 reminds us: Jesus Christ is the same yesterday, today, and forever. Take a few moments to share these reflections with your spouse.

💬 *As I reflect on Jesus with outstretched arms, welcoming me as he did Zacchaeus, I . . .*

 L4. A Spirit-empowered disciple lives joyfully and confidently in his identity as one who is loved by God and belongs to him.

Personal Application

Reflecting again on our physical, spiritual, and relational needs provides an important insight into the marriage intimacy journey. We are called to love our partner physically, spiritually, and relationally. When there is closeness and oneness in all three dimensions, marriages thrive!

DIMENSIONS OF MARRIAGE INTIMACY

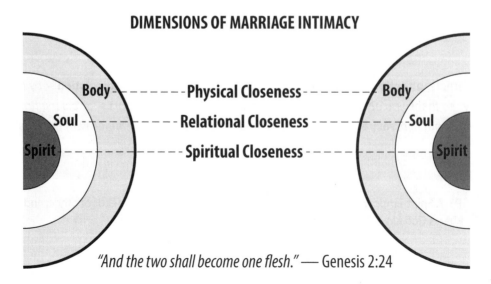

"And the two shall become one flesh." — Genesis 2:24

Think about each of the three dimensions of marriage intimacy: physical, spiritual and relational. Share one way you would like to increase closeness in one of these dimensions. Share truthfully, but in love. Be sure to use the sentence starter below.

Speak the truth in love.

EPHESIANS 4:15

 I am looking forward to us (for example, holding hands more often, dating more, praying more together) . . .

W4. A Spirit-empowered disciple regularly and vulnerably shares with others how God's Word is making a difference.

CALLED 2 LOVE MEANS:

- Exploring important relational needs in the midst of life events.

- Giving to the relational needs of others.

MARRIAGE INTIMACY IS DEEPENED AS YOU CONTINUE DOING THE BIBLE AND EXPERIENCING:

- Ephesians 1:16 – Giving thanks for and mentioning your spouse in prayer.

- Matthew 10:8 – Freely giving to the needs of your spouse.

- Ephesians 4:15 – Sharing truth in love.

YOUR RELATIONSHIP WITH JESUS IS DEEPENED AS YOU:

- Imagine Jesus accepting you just as you are.

- Meditate often and imagine Jesus accepting you and welcoming you just as you are (Luke 19:5; Romans 15:7).

The Mystery of Connection

And if one member suffers, all the members suffer with it;
if one member is honored, all the members rejoice with it.

1 CORINTHIANS 12:26 NASB

Our *Called 2 Love* journey will lead us into the divine mystery of connectedness with both our spouse and our Lord.

Loving like Jesus involves sensing God's multi-faceted love and how he is giving to your partner. Loving like Jesus means asking him to teach you how he loves your spouse and then joining Jesus in expressing that kind of love. When Jesus is encouraging your partner, join him; when he's comforting your partner, add your comfort as well.

This mystery highlights the importance of seeing your spouse as God sees him or her, so that you can love your spouse the way God does. Ask the Lord to give you an attentive heart. Ask him to show you how he cares for your spouse and pray that his Spirit will prompt and empower you to join him.

Let's join the Fergusons as they show us how their marriage journey led them into this mystery.

Teach Me How to Love

As I transitioned into pastoral ministry, I understood what Scripture taught about my relationship with Teresa, but I did not understand that I needed Christ's Spirit to empower his love for my wife.

The first of a number of passages God used to confirm this in me was 1 Peter 3:7. "Husbands, you in turn must treat your wives with tenderness, viewing them as feminine partners who deserve to be honored, for they are co-heirs with you of the 'divine grace of life,' so that nothing will hinder your prayers" (TPT). As this verse penetrated my heart, I remember thinking: *My oneness with God is integrally related to oneness with my wife!*

God emphasized this point to me one evening as Teresa and I were hosting a Bible study in our home. On this particular evening, we were discussing how our concept of God is often shaped by our childhood experiences. I asked the people in the circle to share an early memory about their fathers. We went all the way around the circle, each person sharing memories. Many were positive, and some were painful.

Finally, it was Teresa's turn. She told a story I had never heard before. Here it is, in her words.

"With six children in our home, sometimes my (Teresa) parents didn't seem to have enough attention to go around. To complicate matters, three of my siblings were hearing impaired, requiring special attention. So as a five-year-old, I remember craving my daddy's attention and being disappointed when he had so little left for me. Every evening just before Dad arrived home from work, I got very anxious. I remember thinking, 'Maybe Daddy will play with me when he gets home tonight.' Yet he rarely did, and I often went to bed in tears."

"One Saturday morning I woke up early, realizing that Daddy didn't have to go to work that day. My brothers and sisters were not awake yet, so I wandered through the quiet house looking for my dad. He was not inside, so I went outside, first to the front yard then around to the back. I finally noticed him on top of the house, getting ready to put on a new roof. As usual, he didn't notice me watching him. I remember going to the ladder and climbing it in my nightgown and house shoes. Rung by rung, I made it to the top of the roof—a very scary activity for a five-year-old. Incredibly, I looked past the fear because this was my chance for Daddy's attention. I just wanted to be with him."

As Teresa shared her touching story, something profound began to happen in me. I (David) began to hurt for my wife. Jesus was allowing me to experience the sorrow he felt for Teresa, and I was able to join him. I pulled Teresa to me, wept for her, and confessed my part in adding to her pain, because I, too, often missed meeting her need for attention. That day, I saw Teresa like Jesus saw her and committed to love her the way he loved her.

Pause and think about how Jesus sees your partner. How might his/her life experiences inform your love?

♥ Pause and claim the promise of Jeremiah 33:3 related to your spouse and marriage: "Call to Me and I will answer you, and I will tell you great and mighty things, which you do not know" (NASB).

What might God want to let you know about your spouse? How might Jesus want you to join him in loving your partner well? Take a few moments to ask him: *"Heavenly Father, what is it about my spouse and marriage that I need to know? Give me the power and ability to love like you do."*

Life brings inevitable pain. That means your partner has experienced his or her share of hurt. Scripture is clear that the "God of all comfort" ministers compassion to your spouse. He invites you to join him in giving that same comfort (2 Corinthians 1:3–4 NASB).

Pause and imagine the times of sadness, loss, and aloneness that your partner has experienced. Ask the Holy Spirit to empower your compassion and bless your spouse with the gift of comfort. Ask him to help you live out the promise of Matthew 5:4.

Just a few simple words are powerful demonstrations of care: *"I'm so sorry you went through that. I feel sad because I love you."* Consider Jesus' words: "Blessed are those who mourn, for they shall be comforted" (Matthew 5:4 NASB).

DAY 16

Manage Your Emotions or They Will Manage You!

"But the things that proceed out of the mouth come from the heart, and those defile the man."

MATTHEW 15:18 NASB

When relational needs go unmet, bad things happen. Unhealed pain accumulates. How do we resolve the inevitable hurt, anger, or fear that are a part of life? God's Word provides truth that sets us free! Experiencing these biblical truths can be a challenge because we often seem to ignore our pain or attack others in the midst of the pain. Living out our call to love means actually doing the Bible verses that bring healing, renewed hope, and deepened closeness.

Read one of David's stories next. It illustrates that God has not left us in a pain-filled world without truth, which sets us free. God has also provided his Spirit, who empowers healing!

The Priority of Healing Emotions

Andy was a very large, very angry forty-year-old man. Although he had recently become a follower of Jesus, Andy had a history of violence that often got him into trouble. Before his visit with me (David), Andy even spent time in jail for physically abusing his wife and kids.

During a second time of marital separation, Andy's pastor confronted him, and the church leaders insisted on some counseling for Andy, so the pastor made the call. "David, I'm at the end of my wits with Andy. We have prayed together on numerous occasions about his anger. I sense his genuine desire to change and find freedom. He has made much progress, but both he and I are fearful of the future. I have counseled him from Scripture, and he is involved in a men's accountability group. But I still sense a reservoir of rage just below the surface. Nothing seems to help. I'm afraid Andy might hurt someone again. Will you please talk to him?" I said I would see Andy if the pastor came along. He agreed.

When the two men walked in, Andy was noticeably irritated. It was clear that he didn't want to be there. "Andy, your pastor has filled me in on your background, and I have read about some of the things you have experienced. I am happy about your recent confessions and affirm your desire to get freedom from your anger. Yet, I want to tell you something else I know about you. I know that underneath the anger and rage that have ruled your life for so many years, you are really hurting."

Andy's face softened, as if the anger was being drained from him. I continued, "In fact, when I think about the magnitude of abuse that has poured out of your life, I'm convinced that there is an enormous amount of pain, hurt, and fear inside you, and you have been dealing with it all alone."

When I said the word *alone*, tears came to Andy's eyes. I said, "You know the pain is in there, don't you, Andy? You've been dealing with it alone, haven't you?"

He nodded in agreement as tears started to roll down his cheeks.

"You know that Pastor Clint loves you, don't you, Andy?"

He nodded again, indicating that he did. At this point in our time together, Andy had not spoken a word to me—but the Great Physician was at work.

"Andy, I'm going to slip out of the room for a few minutes. The Bible says that God is the God of all comfort. There are times when God wants to give us some of his comfort delivered through other people. If you are willing, I'd like you to move over beside your pastor and just begin telling him about the hurt that has been inside you for so long. Let your friend hurt with you. Would you be willing to do that?"

Andy finally spoke and said that he would.

I prayed with them briefly and then left the room. During the twenty minutes that I was gone, Andy wept and poured out three decades of deep hurt. When I returned, Clint and Andy were on their knees embracing. They had just finished praying together.

At Clint's encouragement, Andy told me part of his story.

When Andy was nine-years-old, he was running home one night because he was late for curfew. He took a shortcut through the park, and some men stepped out of the darkness and grabbed him. Those men sexually abused the terrified boy and then let him go.

When Andy finally got home, he took his punishment for being late and never told his parents about the incident in the park. For thirty years, Andy had carried his pain and shame alone, blaming himself for the humiliating abuse he had suffered. "None of it would have happened," he had told himself repeatedly, "if I had not been late."

Andy rose from his knees that day with a great burden lifted, and a new perspective on his life as a follower of Jesus.

This was only one step in Andy's journey of healing, but it was a very important step. His wife later offered her tear-filled comfort, and Andy experienced even more sorrow over how he had hurt her and his children. Through these times of comfort and confession, the Great Physician did an even deeper healing in Andy and his family. The Lord faithfully completed that work because today Andy and his wife lead a team of couples who help other couples experience God's intimacy and abundance in their marriages.

Pause and dream about how your relationship would change if God's Spirit brought healing to life's pain.

*When Jesus therefore saw her weeping, and the
Jews who came with her also weeping,
He was deeply moved in spirit and was troubled. Jesus wept.*

JOHN 11:33, 35 NASB

We have been given the Holy Spirit as our *Comforter. He* will move us with compassion, just like he did with Jesus. We can count on him to help us express caring compassion toward those we love, beginning with our spouse. Ask God to empower you to live out Romans 12:15b, "Mourn with those who mourn":

God, I'm asking you to move my heart with your compassion, beginning with my spouse.

♥ God's lovingkindness can bring you freedom to care for others. Claim the promise of Psalm 40:11 — "You, O Lord, will not withhold Your compassion from me; Your lovingkindness and Your truth will continually preserve me" (NASB).

DAY 17

Created with Emotions

I will give thanks to You, for I am fearfully and wonderfully made;
Wonderful are Your works, And my soul knows it very well.

PSALM 139:14 NASB

Your emotions are not a surprise to the Lord. He made you and knows you intimately. Dealing with your emotions and healing them according to God's truth is critical to marriage intimacy.

God made each of us in his image and after his likeness (Genesis 1:26). That means we experience all kinds of painful emotions just as Jesus did. The Savior is described as "a man of sorrows, acquainted with deepest grief," but he is also a great High Priest who can sympathize with us and our emotions (Isaiah 53:3; Hebrews 4:15). Jesus experienced many of the same painful emotions we experience:

- There were times when Christ was disappointed. Remember when his disciples failed to see or understand the Savior's identity (John 13:10)?

- Jesus experienced anger because of the Pharisees' blindness to truth (Mark 3:5).

- Christ felt the pain of aloneness when the disciples fell asleep during his darkest hour (Matthew 26:36–46).

Next, read the Uhlmann's story and how they were challenged to find freedom and healing from painful emotions.

Trust the Journey

I (Barbara) was on a journey to discover the beauty and worth of who I really was so I could love Steve as I loved myself. That discovery would lead me to face my unhealed emotions. That was somewhat of a frightening thought to me. Yet Steve and Linda were there to gently guide me as I was challenged to explore my childhood pain.

The apostle Paul spoke about how we are to deal with our childhood. He wrote, "When I was a child, I talked like a child, I thought like a child, I reasoned like a child. When I became a [mature] man, I put the ways of childhood behind me" (1 Corinthians 13:11 NIV). In other words, he grew up. That's what becoming mature spiritually and emotionally is all about. He went on to write, "we will be mature in the Lord, measuring up to the full and complete standard of Christ. Then we will no longer be immature like children" (Ephesians 4:13, 14).

•••

Barbara needed to connect with the emotions of her childhood so she could, in a real sense, allow that part of herself to get "unstuck" and become mature. It seemed strange to me (Steve) at first that she needed to visit her childhood pain to connect with herself. My approach was to just leave it in the past and move on.

Somehow Barbara was getting to the bottom of things, and if it meant a little self-talk to get there, so be it. The whole process got me to question if my "leave it in the past" approach was working for me. As I began to think about some of my childhood pain, perhaps I needed some healing too. I began to wonder if that was a key aspect to maturity.

•••

As Linda was encouraging me (Barbara) to face the hurts of my past, she helped me realize that it was the childlike part of me that was wounded most.

"When you try to think of the memories of what you experienced as a child," Linda began, "why don't you write it out in your journal? And when you do, write those feelings *with your left hand.*"

"But I'm right handed," I explained.

"I know. But let your left hand express your childlike voice and your right hand be your adult voice. Let's just try it."

I was skeptical at first, but it worked. By changing hands, I was somehow able to engage my memories differently. My left handwriting was unsteady and looked similar to a child's writing. However, the real goal was to explore emotions that I had buried so many years before. The idea was to give a voice to whatever pain and frustrations I felt. No emotions were off limits, and no frustration was to be ignored.

One of the most important parts of the exercise involved recognizing that God really wanted me to tell him how I was feeling. I found the words from the apostle Peter most encouraging. "Give all your worries and cares to God, for he cares about you" (1 Peter 5:7).

With God as my strength and Linda as my guide, I ventured into the memories of some pain-filled moments.

I wrote in my journal:

> August 14
>
> *Yesterday, when I got home from physical therapy, I called Steve to tell him about my low blood sugar attack. I thought he might want to come home and be with me. He was busy helping a friend put siding on a playhouse. I could tell he didn't want to leave—so I told him I was feeling better when I actually wasn't. That moment felt like so many others I had experienced as a child.*
>
> *I would describe my feelings now as an adult and then as a child:*
> *I feel sad, left behind, resentful, insecure, afraid, unimportant, useless, pitied, weary, wrung-out, tired, betrayed, lonely, cheated, helpless, confused, afraid, rejected, unwanted, and frustrated.*

That was an early encounter with the childhood memories. It was an overload of feelings that were being expressed. I didn't know exactly where they were coming from, but I needed to trust God with each emotion. He created me with these emotions, but I needed to learn what to do with them.

Pause and reflect on the painful emotions your spouse might struggle with at times.

Search me, O God, and know my heart; Try me and know my anxious thoughts;
And see if there be any hurtful way in me, And lead me in the everlasting way.

PSALM 139:23–24 NASB

On this marriage intimacy journey, it is important that we deal with our emotions biblically, **not ignore them.** For example, we are instructed to "get rid of all bitterness, rage, anger" and told that "perfect love expels all fear" (Ephesians 4:31–32; 1 John 4:18–19).

Father, you know my heart and my emotions. Help me understand them and heal any emotions that need healing according to your Word.

God, you know my spouse's heart and emotions. Please give me more sensitivity and compassion for _____ because he/she feels _____ at times.

♥ Claim the promise of Deuteronomy 30:15–16: "See, I have set before you today life and prosperity, and death and adversity; in that I command you today to love the Lord your God, to walk in His ways and to keep His commandments and His statutes and His judgments, that you may live and multiply, and that the Lord your God may bless you in the land where you are entering to possess it" (NASB).

WEEK THREE

71

DAY 18

Pour Out Your Heart

On God my salvation and my glory rest;
The rock of my strength, my refuge is in God.
Trust in Him at all times, O people; Pour out your heart before Him;
God is a refuge for us. Selah.

PSALM 62:7–8 NASB

The Psalmist reminds us to pour out our heart to the Lord and to embrace the real God as One who is a place of refuge and safety.

If there is one thing we can learn from the story of King David and the writers of all the Psalms, it's that it is ok to be real with God—especially since he already knows our heart!

Think about your own marriage as you read the story from the Uhlmanns. Let it sink in how beneficial it was for Barbara to pour out more and more of her heart.

God Is a Refuge for Our Emotions

The panic attacks, chronic fatigue, and then a later battle with cancer and chemotherapy took a heavy toll on my body. At times, I (Barbara) didn't know how I could go on. Intense and consistent pain is wearing physically and emotionally. It challenged me spiritually too.

Through all the suffering, I began experincing God in a new way. He became more real to me each day I suffered. I was learning that the God-man, Jesus, understood what suffering was like. While on earth, he experienced ridicule, rejection, abandonment, misunderstanding, and betrayal.

A new view of God was emerging. I was sharing my emotions with a caring and kind God, one who said, "I will never fail you. I will never abandon you" (Hebrews 13:5). He wanted me to be open and real to him. He was becoming my special safe place. On June 25th, I wrote in my journal:

> *Lord, I give you my anxiety, my hurt, my insecurity, my frustration, my confusion, my fear, my weariness, my feeling of being forgotten. You have told us to cast all our anxieties and cares on you, for you care for us. If I am to continue to suffer, Lord, it is to get a taste of your suffering. I am trusting you to give me the strength and perseverance to get through each day. I want to glorify you even through this time.*

During that time, the following four verses took on new meaning to me:

- Be merciful to me, O Lord, for I am in distress; my eyes grow weak with sorrow, my soul and my body with grief. My life is consumed by anguish and my years by groaning; my strength fails because of my affliction, and my bones grow weak (Psalm 31:9–10 NIV).
- But as for me, I watch in hope for the Lord. I wait for God my Savior, my God will hear me (Micah 7:7 NIV).
- My flesh and my heart may fail, but God is the strength of my heart and my portion forever (Psalm 73:26 NIV).
- I will be glad and rejoice in your unfailing love, for you have seen my troubles, and you care about the anguish of my soul (Psalm 31:7).

Before, I would only hear verses like these with my rational mind. They would not reach deep into my emotions. Now they were becoming healing words from God applied to the painful feelings of the past. I was slowly learning how Father God's love was an accepting love that I could count on. He truly loved all of me and was a safe place for me to be real.

 Pause and imagine the God of all comfort listening and being a safe place for all of your emotions.

The name of the Lord is a strong tower;
The righteous runs into it and is safe.

PROVERBS 18:10 NASB

First, pause and celebrate that the God of the universe cares for *you*, no matter the condition of your heart. He is your refuge and safe place, because he is the God of all comfort.

Lord Jesus, I celebrate that I can trust you with my heart, thoughts, emotions, and hopes. I trust in you for compassion, freedom, and healing. I am especially grateful that . . .

Secondly, it is important to remember that we are to be good stewards of God's comfort. Pause and imagine the God of all comfort comforting you. Now imagine him giving you the strength, ability, and power to comfort your spouse.

♥ Ask the Lord to make this promise real for you: "Blessed be the God and Father of our Lord Jesus Christ, the Father of mercies and God of all comfort, who comforts us in all our affliction so that we will be able to comfort those who are in any affliction with the comfort with which we ourselves are comforted by God" (2 Corinthians 1:3–4 NASB).

DAY 19

What Needs to Be Healed?

Making It Personal

The words of the wise bring healing.

PROVERBS 12:18

Remember this principle from our previous day's devotional? When relational needs are met, good things happen. When relational needs go unmet, bad things can happen. One of those bad things is that we feel something. We feel painful emotions.

Additionally, any time that we struggle to embrace our identity as "God's beloved," we can often trace this struggle back to unhealed emotional pain.

Just like the Uhlmanns and Fergusons, we can accumulate pain as we go through life. The diagram on page 78 illustrates how painful emotions can build and lead to destructive symptoms. These symptoms steal our joy and cloud our identity as the "beloved of God."

WHAT PAIN NEEDS TO BE HEALED?

Let's take a look at different kinds of painful emotions and how to heal them. When we focus on healing the painful emotions of our lives, we gain freedom to experience more positive emotions, find life fulfillment, experience more productive behaviors, and enjoy a more intimate marriage.

To start the healing process, we must first focus on "What pain needs to be healed?" When we prioritize healing painful emotions, we avoid wasting energy trying to manage the symptoms that "spill out" of our emotional cup. When painful emotions are healed, we experience more joy and freedom in our personal lives and in our marriage.

We start our healing by looking at the emotion of hurt. We've all experienced this emotion because every person on the planet has felt some kind of rejection, disappointment, disconnection, aloneness, ridicule, neglect, or abuse. These feelings can grip our hearts with sadness and sorrow, even if we have ignored them for years.

This relational and emotional hurt can lead to:

- **Anger** toward those who have hurt us.

- **Guilt** because of our own unproductive or less-than-Christlike responses.

- **Fear** that we might be hurt in the future.

- **Condemnation** that can be added to our emotional cup. This emotion can be described as an overall sense of unworthiness and can hinder our ability to embrace our true identity as the beloved of God. Condemnation can be the result of abuse or neglect, when we receive rejection rather than acceptance, coldness rather than affection, or neglect rather than support.

THE EMOTIONAL CUP

When relational needs go unmet, they often bring one or more of these primary painful emotions:

Loss of energy or concentration

Depressed mood

Impatience, quick temper

Controlling behaviors, obsessive-compulsive, anxiety, insecurity

Escaping into work, social media, infidelity, pornography, entertainment, TV, computer, etc.

Physical Effects:
sleep/appetite disturbances, headaches stomachaches, digestive problems, overeating

Loss of positive emotions like peace, love and gratitude

WHAT EMPTIES THE CUP?			BIBLICAL ANTIDOTES
	POSITIVE EMOTIONS		
Truth ▶	CONDEMNATION	◀	Romans 8:1
Admit you were wrong Ask forgiveness ▶	GUILT	◀	1 John 1:9 James 5:16
Reassurance demonstrated by commitment, support or needed change ▶	FEAR	◀	1 John 4:18 2 Timothy 1:7
Speak truth, forgiveness ▶	ANGER, RESENTMENT	◀	Ephesians 4:31, 32 Proverbs 15:1
Grieve the hurt, receive comfort/care ▶	HURT, SADNESS, DISAPPOINTMENT	◀	Romans 12:15b Matthew 5:4

RELATIONAL NEEDS *UNMET* OFTEN BRING ONE OR MORE OF THESE PAINFUL EMOTIONS.
THIS DECREASES OUR CAPACITY FOR POSITIVE EMOTION AND OFTEN RESULTS IN UNHEALTHY SYMPTOMS.

UNMET RELATIONAL NEEDS = PAIN

My Personal Story

WHAT'S IN YOUR CUP?

If we are going to be aware of how emotions play a significant role in our life and marriage, it makes sense that we first examine our own emotions. In addition to the positive emotions that are present in your emotional cup, consider some of the more painful feelings as well. Circle some of the positive and painful emotions you have felt in recent months.

Angry	Ticked-off	Forgiven	Disgusted
Furious	Insecure	Carefree	Frustrated
Antagonistic	Oppressed	Generous	Insulted
Resentful	Burdened	Compassionate	Restless
Spiteful	Sad	Anxious	Jumpy
Vengeful	Lonely	Shy	Betrayed
Nervous	Dumb	Worried	Aloof
Jittery	Cherished	Tense	Grateful
Exasperated	Desirable	Arrogant	Confident
Irritable	Free	Cowardly	Accepted
Bewildered	Attractive	Weary	Worthwhile
Bored	Suicidal	Humiliated	Important
Depressed	Ugly	Small	Fit
Unimportant	Picked-on	Hurt	Lighthearted
Belittled	Harassed	Happy	Disappointed
Confused	Wary	Joyful	Afraid
Out-of-it	Inadequate	Excited	Apprehen-sive
Terrified	Useless	Magnanimous	
Frightened	Violated	Loved	Guilty
Suffocated	Haughty	Awed	Embarrassed
Trapped	Pitied	Humble	Unfulfilled
Lost	Foolish	Bold	Empty
Uptight	Cheated	Hopeful	Overwhelmed
Bitter	Old	Uncomfortable	Wrung-out
Tricked	Talkative	Rejected	Strong
Deceived	Helpless	Unwanted	Weak

Recently, I have felt _____ *when* _____

_____

_____

_____

My Marriage Story

What Symptoms Would We See?

As your emotional cup gets full of difficult or painful emotions, what spills out—especially in your marriage relationship? How does your pain get revealed in outward behavior? What does it look like when your emotional cup is full? (Need a hint? These symptoms are very often points of conflict or concern in your marriage.)

Symptoms

- Difficulty sleeping
- Escaping into TV, work, busyness, social media
- Irritability and impatience
- Perfectionism and controlling behaviors
- Self-demeaning comments
- Physical complaints (headaches, stomachaches, rashes, etc.)
- Loss of joy and other positive emotions
- Increased activity/burnout
- Chronic fatigue
- Overeating/loss of appetite
- Dependency on drugs and/or alcohol
- Over-thinking, obsessive worry
- Depression

Circle as many of the symptoms listed above that apply to you.

When I am emotionally stressed out and my emotional cup seems full, I might experience . . .

Jesus Comes to Find Us!

He rides across the heavens to help you.

DEUTERONOMY 33:26

My Jesus Story

Christ commanded us to love our neighbor and to love as he loves (Matthew 22:37–40; John 13:34). He also reminded us that love is from God and that anyone who does not love must not know God. If we have difficulty loving those nearest us—especially our spouse—it is often connected to the fact that we don't *know the real God*. You see, our view of God impacts our ability to love him and other people.

Our perspective of God has been shaped by certain life events, the religious experiences we've encountered, and by our own growing up. One way to begin seeing the real God is to know and experience Christ's heart toward our pain. He hurts for us and can't wait to care when he sees us go through life's struggles.

Be sure to read the Bible passage that reminds us of Christ's heart for us. John 9:1–41 beautifully reveals the real God.

His Story

When Jesus learned they had thrown him out,
he went to find him.

JOHN 9:35 TPT

THE MAN BORN BLIND

In John 9:1–41, the gospel tells us about a man who was born without sight, abandoned by his family, and rejected by the religious leaders. The man born blind undoubtedly experienced an incredible amount of painful emotion.

In the midst of these hurtful moments, we read one of the most comforting declarations of God's heart toward us. "*He went to find him . . .*" This simple statement in the gospel story reminds us: we have a God who will find us—a God who hears, notices, and cares about our pain.

Hebrews 13:8 tells us that Jesus is the same today as he was two thousand years ago. Therefore, we can be assured that just as Jesus took initiative to care for the man born blind, the Savior hears and notices our pain, and he comes to find us too. Our painful emotions move his heart to care. Our God is a safe place for us to be real, authentic, and vulnerable.

Your Jesus Story

The Gospel of John describes the best day in the blind man's life, and yet no one—not friends, family, or the religious community—was willing to celebrate with him. The people of the neighborhood ignored the man. The religious leaders accused him. His family rejected him.

Just like we do, the unnamed man suffered from:

- Painful life events—he was born blind.
- Unsupportive relationships—his loved ones seemed neglectful and rejecting.
- Irrelevant religion—legalistic Pharisees threw him out of the synagogue.

Here's the amazing news of this passage. When Jesus heard about the man's painful life events, he went to find the man! Imagine this. Because Jesus is the same today as he was two thousand years ago, our Savior's heart is moved by the struggles of your life too.

Pause quietly to reflect on some of your own painful experiences.

- What life events have been hurtful? What losses have you experienced?
- What relationships have been hurtful?
- What religious experiences have been painful or irrelevant?

Some of the painful moments I've had include . . .

Imagine Jesus learning of your hurtful experiences and coming to find you!

Now meditate and give thanks for Jesus because he notices you, comes to find you, and cares for the hurts of your life (John 9:35).

Jesus, I am grateful you notice and care about me. I'm grateful for the truth that you pursue me because . . .

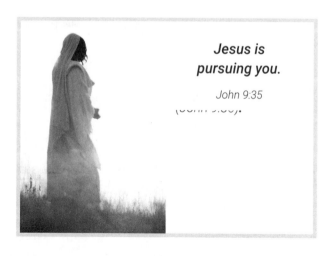

Jesus is pursuing you.

John 9:35

Sharing Your Week 3 Journey

The Lord is good to everyone. He showers compassion on all his creation.

PSALM 145:9

Marriage Staff Meeting

In this Marriage Staff Meeting, you will talk to your spouse about some of the painful emotions you have each experienced. You will have the opportunity to identify some of the symptoms that are true when your emotional cup is full. Be ready to be vulnerable but never accusing. This is the time to share your own struggles, not your partner's. You'll have the chance to gently let your spouse know the things that he or she can do that are helpful when you're stressed and emotions are running high. It's a great chance to talk through the do's and don'ts of conflict when tensions are low.

You will spend some time sharing about your moments with Jesus and his compassionate, pursuing love. Be sure to celebrate the incredible comfort this brings.

Finally, you and your partner will have the tremendous privilege to join Jesus in comforting your spouse. This can be one of the most sacred moments of your marriage.

Share with humility and sincerity. Ask God to move your heart with compassion for your spouse and then let the words you say match your heart.

Share Your Personal Story

Which emotions have you felt in recent months?

🗨 *Recently, I have felt _____ when . . .*

🗨 *When I am emotionally stressed out and my emotional cup seems full, the symptoms you might see in my life include . . .*

Share Your Marriage Stories

🗨 *During the times when my emotional cup is full, it is helpful for my spouse to . . .*

Share Your Reflections from Your Jesus Stories

As the story of the man born blind revealed, Jesus pursues us in our pain. He comes to look for us when we hurt.

It's also important to remember that Jesus comes to us with a compassionate heart. Jesus comforted people throughout his time on earth. On the eve of his own death, Jesus comforted the disciples because he sensed their sorrow and anxiety (John 14:1, 18, 27; 16:3). The Bible also reminds us there were even times when Jesus identified with others' pain to such an extent that he wept for them (John 11:35; Luke 19:41). Jesus was moved deeply as he wept with his friends, Mary and Martha. Their loss filled his heart with such compassion that the Savior couldn't help but cry with them.

Jesus wept.

JOHN 11:35

Consider this: "Jesus Christ is the same yesterday and today and forever" (Hebrews 13:8 NASB). This means that the same Jesus who cried for Mary's pain still hurts for his friends today. The Jesus who was moved to tears because of Mary's loss is the same Jesus who is moved with compassion for you. Your painful experiences, your moments of hurt and loss move Christ's heart, and he hurts—for you!

Take the next few moments to praise the God of all comfort for pursuing you and sharing some of his comfort with you. He sees your hurt but doesn't lecture, criticize, compare, give pep talks, or neglect. Jesus, who is the same yesterday, today, and forever, weeps when you weep. Praise him in prayer and then share your responses with your spouse.

 When I imagine that Jesus pursues me, sees my hurt, and is moved with compassion, I feel incredibly grateful because . . .

Just as Jesus loves and comforts you, he calls you to comfort others, beginning with your spouse. This will be our focus next.

Grace to you and peace from God our Father and the Lord Jesus Christ. Blessed be the God and Father of our Lord Jesus Christ, the Father of mercies and God of all comfort, who comforts us in all our affliction so that we will be able to comfort those who are in any affliction with the comfort with which we ourselves are comforted by God.

2 CORINTHIANS 1:2–4 NASB

SPIRIT EMPOWERED Faith L3. A Spirit-empowered disciple develops a correct view of God as the Lord reveals himself; enjoying more and more closeness with him.

Doing the Bible

Weep with those who weep.

ROMANS 12:15B

One additional truth we learn from John 11 is revealed in what Jesus *didn't* say to his friends. We know that compassion for Mary and Martha flowed out of the God of all comfort, but let's consider what Jesus *could have* said to his friends. Thankfully, Christ refrained from these unhelpful responses.

These unproductive responses miss the mark in relationships. Think about how these unproductive responses have produced a communication gap in your own marriage.

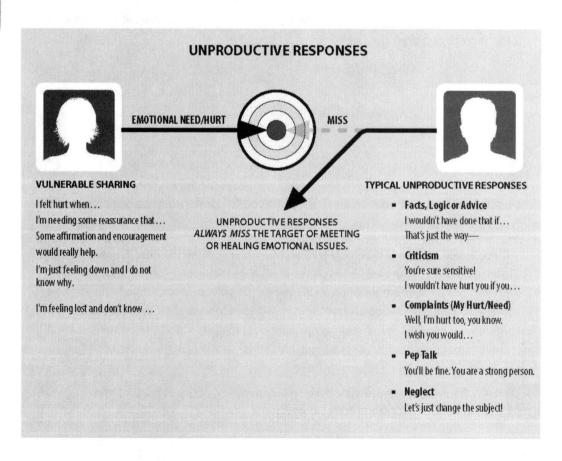

UNPRODUCTIVE RESPONSES

EMOTIONAL NEED/HURT

MISS

VULNERABLE SHARING

I felt hurt when...

I'm needing some reassurance that...

Some affirmation and encouragement would really help.

I'm just feeling down and I do not know why.

I'm feeling lost and don't know ...

UNPRODUCTIVE RESPONSES
ALWAYS MISS THE TARGET OF MEETING
OR HEALING EMOTIONAL ISSUES.

TYPICAL UNPRODUCTIVE RESPONSES

- **Facts, Logic or Advice**
  I wouldn't have done that if...
  That's just the way—

- **Criticism**
  You're sure sensitive!
  I wouldn't have hurt you if you...

- **Complaints (My Hurt/Need)**
  Well, I'm hurt too, you know.
  I wish you would...

- **Pep Talk**
  You'll be fine. You are a strong person.

- **Neglect**
  Let's just change the subject!

Jesus could have given:

- **Advice or instruction:** "Let me tell you how to solve this problem."

- **Logic or reasoning:** "Let's analyze the situation and I'll tell you why this happened."

- **A pep talk:** "Everything is going to be alright! Tomorrow will be a better day!"

- **Criticism:** "You've got to have more faith!"

- **Complaint:** "It could be worse. At least, you have each other."

- **Spiritualization:** "God is going to work this out for your good!"

Just as Jesus refrained from these unhelpful responses, we want to do the same. Any time someone is hurting, we want the God of all comfort to prompt and empower us to leave the unhelpful responses behind and share words of compassion.

The chart below details what words of comfort might sound like.

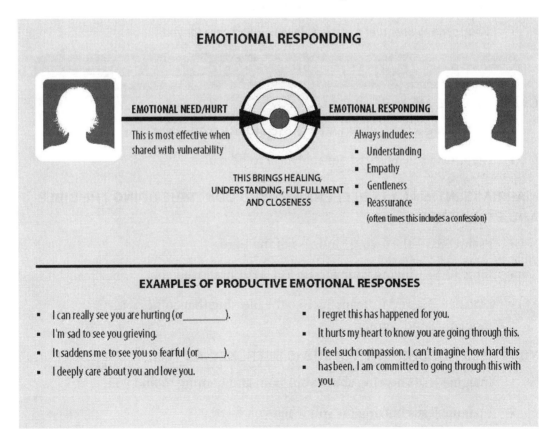

EMOTIONAL RESPONDING

EMOTIONAL NEED/HURT

This is most effective when shared with vulnerability

THIS BRINGS HEALING, UNDERSTANDING, FULFULLMENT AND CLOSENESS

EMOTIONAL RESPONDING

Always includes:
- Understanding
- Empathy
- Gentleness
- Reassurance
  (often times this includes a confession)

EXAMPLES OF PRODUCTIVE EMOTIONAL RESPONSES

- I can really see you are hurting (or_____).
- I'm sad to see you grieving.
- It saddens me to see you so fearful (or_____).
- I deeply care about you and love you.

- I regret this has happened for you.
- It hurts my heart to know you are going through this.
- I feel such compassion. I can't imagine how hard this has been. I am committed to going through this with you.

Pause for a moment and live out your calling to love like Jesus by mourning with those who who mourn (Romans 12:15b).

Take turns reflecting on a time of significant sadness, sorrow, or loss *that your partner did not cause.* (You might want to think about hurt from friendships, extended family, work relationships, childhood, or any other emotional pain outside the marriage relationship.) Share these responses with your partner.

I remember feeling alone/sad/disappointed when . . .

After your partner talks about their hurt, love them like Jesus. Avoid any of the unproductive responses. Instead, share words of comfort like these:

- *I'm so sorry that happened . . .*
- *I'm sad you had to go through that . . .*
- *I feel a lot of compassion for you because . . .*
- *It hurts me to hear that because I love you and care for you.*

HERE'S A SUMMARY OF YOUR WEEK 3 JOURNEY

CALLED 2 LOVE MEANS:

- Embracing a God who can be trusted to listen and care.
- Creating a safe place in our marriage to be real.

MARRIAGE INTIMACY IS DEEPENED AS YOU CONTINUE DOING THE BIBLE AND EXPERIENCE:

- Psalm 63:3—the loving kindness of the Lord.
- John 13:34—loving your spouse as Christ has loved you.
- Matthew 5:4 and Romans 12:15—the blessing that comes with mourning and comfort.

YOUR RELATIONSHIP WITH JESUS IS DEEPENED AS YOU:

- Imagine Jesus hearing about your pain and coming to find you.
- Imagine Jesus hurting for you when you hurt.

DAY 22

The Journey from Head to Heart

Godly sorrow brings repentance.

2 CORINTHIANS 7:10 NIV

Everyone fights the battle of turning what we believe and know into heartfelt living.

- Gentle words really do achieve better results than harsh words, but a gentle response can be hard to live out in a relationship (Proverbs 15:1).

- We have been called to impart our life and the gospel, but sharing our faith in Jesus can be one of the hardest things we do (1 Thessalonians 2:8–9).

- Children are gifts from the Lord, but sometimes it's difficult to see and relate to them in a way that matches what we believe (Psalm 127:3).

Turning our beliefs into behavior is critical to following Jesus and having the abundance in marriage that God intends. At times, we all sense the need and importance of making lasting changes for the betterment of our relationships, but how does true and lasting change happen?

This is the dilemma David faced, but the Father allowed godly sorrow to move from David's head to his heart.

Understanding God's Pain

It happened on a Monday during the desert years of our marriage. Teresa's car was not running, so we only had one car to get me to work and to transport the three children to school. Consequently, we all had to leave together that morning. I quickly got myself ready and went out to wait behind the wheel of the car.

As I sat there, Teresa began a series of trips from the house to the car. She brought out clothes for the dry cleaner and put them in the trunk. She brought out lunches for the children. Next, she appeared with Eric's car seat and put it in the car. Then she brought out Eric, our preschooler, and put him in the car seat. Teresa ushered out our two daughters, and they joined me in the car. That morning I watched Teresa make five or six trips to the car, and never once did it cross my mind, "Why don't you help her?" Rather, the only thought on my mind was, "If she doesn't hurry up, I'm going to honk the horn!"

Teresa describes that time in my life with one word: oblivious. She used to say to me, "David, you are oblivious—your head is always in the clouds. Your kids could be strangling each other right before your eyes, and you would miss it." Teresa was prone to exaggeration, so I thought her assessment was overstated.

Even in my hardheaded impatience that morning, I sensed I had blown it with my wife. When Teresa finally got into the car, I expected either a war of words or her cold shoulder, and I deserved them both.

Yet that morning, a miracle took place. Teresa was patient and kind. God's Spirit was working in her life to help her make the right response to my oblivion that day. She didn't attack me or retreat into cold silence. Instead, as I drove, she talked about the two of us having lunch together that day. She mentioned special weekend plans. I thought I had forfeited all of that with my insensitive behavior.

I had no defense for my wife's kind reply. Had she jumped all over me, I could have fought back with some kind of misguided justification of my behavior. However, Teresa returned good for evil, so when I arrived at the church, I felt terribly guilty. I had good reason to feel that way because I *was* terribly guilty! The kindness of the Lord (demonstrated through Teresa) was slowly bringing repentance to my heart (Romans 2:4).

That's how I began my week: as a minister who is supposed to lead and bless the people of God through a life of personal integrity and as an example of his grace. Wow! I was lacking in both!

As I sat in my office, God began to deal with me. The Holy Spirit seemed to say, "David, Teresa is right. You are oblivious to your wife, your children, and others around you. You are oblivious because you are selfish, preoccupied with your own plans, your own goals, your own agenda, and your own ministry.

I needed to experience 1 John 1:9: "If we confess our sins, He is faithful and righteous to forgive us our sins and to cleanse us from all unrighteousness" (NASB). I had preached on this verse many times. I had studied the word *confession* in the Greek. I knew it meant "to agree with God" or to "say what God says" about my behavior. So I started down the path of confession intellectually and theologically, but my confession was stuck in my head.

God seemed to say, *David, do you really want to confess?* The words of Isaiah 53 suddenly flooded my heart. The Lord was saying, *David, my Son was pierced and crushed because of your selfishness.* Then as I agreed with God that my sin played a role in why his Son had to die, I began to weep. Sitting in my office that day, for the first time, I was experiencing 2 Corinthians 7:10: "Godly sorrow brings repentance."

I sensed the Father's forgiveness, and with it came gratitude and renewed hope. The tears streaming down my face were no longer tears of sorrow but tears of joy and gratitude. I felt joy over God's promise of cleansing and gratitude for his forgiveness. I was truly experiencing 1 John 1:9.

Understanding Your Spouse's Pain

The impact of this time of brokenness in my church office was immediate. I went home to Teresa in the middle of the day and tearfully confessed not only my selfish behavior in the driveway that morning but also a pattern of self-centeredness that had painfully stolen my attention and care from her for many years. A ministry of healing in our marriage began that day as we experienced the promise of James 5:16: "Confess your sins to each other and pray for each other so that you may be healed."

 Pause and imagine the pain that might result in your marriage because your beliefs don't match your behavior.

Consider some issues that seem to resurface in your marriage journey. Maybe you've said, "I'm sorry," or even heard the words "I forgive you," but you realize that true healing has never really occurred. Ask God to reveal unhealed hurt between you and your spouse. "Make your ear attentive to wisdom, incline your heart to understanding" (Proverbs 2:2 NASB). Write about what he reveals.

Father, give me wisdom and an understanding heart to better know my partner and the ways I have hurt him or her in our marriage. Move me with compassion for how I have hurt my partner and you. Change me so that I can better love my spouse.

I sense that God might want me to change in these ways:

♥ Claim the promise of James 5:16 – "Confess your sins . . . that you may be healed."

What's Filling Your Heart?

"A good person produces good things from the treasury of a good heart,
and an evil person produces evil things from the treasury of an evil heart.
What you say flows from what is in your heart."

LUKE 6:45

Healing hurt means healing a heart and healing a marriage!
This wisdom from the Gospel of Luke is certainly true in marriage. Unhealed hurt is like an emotional bruise that your partner may not actually see but that can be incredibly painful to the touch. We can only hide painful feelings for so long. At some point, unhealed pain flows out of our heart and sometimes in ugly ways.

Consider some of the emotional bruises in your own marriage journey as you read another part of the Ferguson's story.

Blessing Comes after Confessing

It was my (David's) birthday, so Teresa invited our extended family over for barbecued steaks. On occasions like this, Teresa slips into a special gear that I humorously refer to as "whip and drive." She sets her mind to getting things organized and getting people fed in the most efficient way possible.

As Teresa hummed along in whip-and-drive mode, I got the big idea that I would help. This was a break from tradition because I don't ever cook. I boldly swaggered into the kitchen and announced, "I'll help with the steaks." I started mixing things into the bowl of sauce that was already prepared and ready to go.

Teresa became unglued. "David, what are you doing?" She barked at me in front of everyone who was in the kitchen. "Leave the barbecue sauce alone, or you'll mess it up."

"Just forget it," I snapped defensively. I slammed the fork onto the counter and retreated out of the kitchen. Not only had Teresa embarrassed me in front of our family, but her reaction had touched some unhealed pain left over from my childhood.

My father was a no-nonsense marine drill sergeant and was just as tough at home as he was with his recruits. While my dad's motives were good, he was often a hard man to please.

When Teresa realized that she had hurt me, she quickly and compassionately responded. Here is her account of what happened after the scene in the kitchen.

"When David tossed the fork and suddenly left the room, I realized how deeply I had wounded him. I was aware of David's painful childhood and knew I had thoughtlessly touched an old wound. At that point, the birthday party and all my preparations were unimportant. I had to make things right with my husband."

"I went into the living room where David was hurting and put my face close to his. Touching his arm, I said with remorse, 'David, I realize how I have just hurt you. I deeply regret the pain I have caused you. It was so wrong of me. Will you forgive me?' David said yes, and we embraced. I was reminded of the fact that just a momentary lapse in my sensitivity can deeply hurt the one I love most. I was also keenly aware that God was working through me to minister an additional measure of healing to David's hurt."

After our guests were gone, Teresa and I dealt more thoroughly with the pain behind my outburst. I explained how her critical remarks seemed to touch a deep sense of rejection and inadequacy in me that I still carried from my growing up.

As Teresa held me and wept with me, my hurt lessened. Teresa and I were acutely aware that something special was happening between us, something beyond the loving words, tender embrace, and tears. We began to understand what Jesus meant when he said, "Blessed are those who mourn, for they will be comforted" (Matthew 5:4 NIV). As I mourned my hurt and received God's comfort through my wife, we were indeed blessed!

Pause and imagine how compassion for your partner's growing-up pain could produce deepened intimacy.

Write down some of the life events and unhealed hurts that your spouse may have brought into your marriage. You may have even encountered some measure of painful emotions and reactions from your partner that had nothing to do with you. You may not be aware of them all, but write down what you know.

♥ Claim the promise of the blessing from Matthew 5:4 — "Blessed are those who mourn, for they will be comforted."

Be open and ready to truly care about your partner's pain and become a channel of God's comfort. Be ready to live out Romans 12:15.

Mourn with those who mourn.

ROMANS 12:15

The Blind Leading the Blind

"You'll grope around in the middle of the day like a blind person feeling his way through a lifetime of darkness; you'll never get to where you're going."

DEUTERONOMY 28:29 MSG

Think back to your wedding day, with all your excitement and hope for an amazing and intimate marriage. Had you ever seen one?

Sadly, many of us, and maybe most of us, have never seen the kind of marriage relationship we hoped for. Instead, we experienced something in our growing up years that was much less than the ideal. Divorce statistics alone seem to prove that marriage is often like the blind leading the blind to a destination neither person has ever seen!

Read this next story in the Uhlmann's journey. It's an amazing testimony of how God's Word and his Spirit can guide us through a lifetime of uncertainty about relationships and get us where we want to go!

Good Was Never Good Enough

Growing up I (Steve) didn't get many positive affirmations from my mother. It seemed all Mom could do is complain about what I didn't do right. I never remember getting a hug from her or hearing her say, "I love you." Rather than feeling I was important to her, it seemed I was more of a nuisance to her than anything else.

Mom was an alcoholic. She was far from being a pleasant woman; in fact, she was quite mean. No one who came in contact with her disputed that.

I remember clearly a day my dad wanted to provide me with a little fun. He had purchased a plastic swimming pool, and I was so excited. He had finished inflating it and was filling it with water.

"Ernest Uhlmann! What in the world are you doing?" Mom yelled from the back porch.

"Steve and I are going to have a little swim party," Dad replied.

"Oh, no you're not," she retorted bolting off the porch yelling obscenities. "It's too cold to have a swim party!"

Before I knew it, my mom was literally jumping on my dad as he attempted to defend himself. After the melee, I vividly remember putting Mercurochrome and Band-Aids on scratches on my dad's back. Mom's verbal and physical abuse of dad was rather commonplace but nevertheless disturbing.

Eventually Dad had enough of her abusive behavior and divorced her. As a child, I envied him more than blamed him. He got away from an abusive wife. I was stuck with an abusive mother.

Even at a young age, work actually became my escape. Dad always praised the work I did. Of course that made me feel good. But while Dad was attempting to teach me the worth of a dollar, I seemed to inadvertently attach my personal worth to my hard work. As a result, I became an overachiever and performance driven. My life was all about achieving and accomplishing things.

Choking on the Pursuit of Success

Barbara and I were high school sweethearts. I had an immediate physical and sexual attraction to her. She was beautiful, and I enjoyed being around her. She was a great listener. She seemed enamored with my ideas and vision for our life together. She was a great champion for what I wanted to do in life and appeared excited about our future. The relationship started off rather one-sided and without much vulnerability, and it pretty much stayed that way.

We were married, and I loved Barbara with the only kind of love I knew—doing things for her. I could do loving things, but I didn't quite know how to love her for being her.

I provided a nice home, clothes, a car, and vacations for my wife. I could do things for her, but beyond that, I didn't know what else to do to express love, except for sex.

The sex was great, but there wasn't a deep emotional connection between us. We were together, but relationally and emotionally, we were alone.

Feeling alone and unfulfilled emotionally in my marriage, I naturally turned to the only thing that I could connect to—my work. It was there that I sought to find my value and worth as a person. Striving to succeed became my passion—the mistress that I ran after day and night.

I knew work wasn't a bad thing and succeeding at what I did wasn't wrong. Yet it seemed I was choking on a pursuit of success that could never bring me the deep love and intimate connection with another person that I needed and wanted.

 Pause and imagine the pain that can be caused in your marriage by being preoccupied with the wrong things.

Serve one another in love.

GALATIANS 5:13

At times, good things like work, hobbies, kid's activities, and even extended family can under-mine the *best* things, like an intimate marriage. Being preoccupied with making a living can hinder us from sharing a deep meaningful life with our partner.

What in your life may have taken too high a priority? Similarly, have you at times "turned to other things" that have been a part of hurting your spouse? Write about those things here.

Now invite the Holy Spirit to speak to you about the things you do and whether they are good or best: *"Holy Spirit, please show me any pain my spouse might experience as I prioritize other people and other pursuits. Refocus my heart on my partner."* Write your prayer here.

♥ Claim the promise of Matthew 7:12 — *"Do to others whatever you would like them to do to you. This is the essence of all that is taught in the law and the prophets."*

WEEK FOUR

DAY 25

The Ways
of the Foolish

Wisdom is enshrined in an understanding heart;
wisdom is not found among fools.

PROVERBS 14:33

At times, every married person has gone down the road of the foolish and brought some kind of pain and distance into the marriage.

Our foolishness may have been in words, attitudes, or actions. There are no perfect people, and that means we've all lacked wisdom and understanding. The good news is: when God's Spirit has his way, he will reveal the foolish ways and show us the path toward righteousness.

Reflect on some of your own foolish ways as you read the Uhlmann's story.

When Our Marriage Was on Autopilot

My (Steve's) growing business was demanding more and more of my attention. That included traveling away from home. At one point, about nine years into our marriage, a business acquaintance introduced me to an escort service, and I became involved with prostitutes. I figured as long as Barbara didn't know about it, no harm done. Intuitively though, Barbara sensed something was wrong. She could feel a greater degree of alienation than already existed between us.

At a conference a few years later, I rededicated my life to Christ. What I confessed to God I also confessed to Barbara. She was devastated. We sought outside help and went through some counseling. My unfaithfulness and betrayal shattered her trust in me.

I promised I would never make contact with prostitutes again, and we tried to move on with life. I kept my promise. From that point on, prostitutes were non-existent in my life, but what took their place was pornography. My attitude toward sex went unchanged, and I was still clueless about how to develop an intimate relationship with Barbara. Our marriage went on autopilot. We cruised along in an atmosphere of shallow unfulfillment for both of us.

When God Became Part of Our Marriage

Barbara's journal:

> December 14
> *I looked at one of those sex books that happened to be on the table this morning, something about how to be a better lover. And I'm feeling inadequate sexually, like I'll never be able to please my husband . . .*

The next day, I mustered up the courage to approach Steve.

"I'd like to talk to you a little bit," I began.

"Sure," Steve responded. "What's up?"

"Well, when I saw that book about how to be a better lover, I sorta reacted negatively. Like I'll never be able to please you."

Steve could sense I was uneasy, so he suggested we sit down and talk it through. Steve said reassuringly, "I want to hear you out and understand where this is coming from, even if it's from my own past failings. Take your time. I want to really know what you are feeling."

My interaction with Steve that day became a defining moment for both of us. In the past, when I alluded to Steve's previous indiscretions, he'd get a little irritated. He figured they were forgiven, so they ought to be forgotten, but not on this day. He seemed to sense a vulnerability from me that got to him. It was like he could see pain mixed with fear in my eyes, and instead of feeling irritated, he was moved deeply.

He sat teary-eyed before me and asked me to share more. He listened as I was able to express the pain I felt from years of neglect, betrayal, inattentiveness, and aloneness. The more deeply he seemed to comprehend my pain, the more deeply he was moved with compassion. Understanding the depth of pain he had contributed to in me seemed to prepare him to offer an emotional, heartfelt confession that I never imagined I would ever hear.

Someone Else Showed Up in the Room

What was happening? I (Steve) was sitting there with Barbara listening to her share emotional pain of which I was the major contributor. It was different this time. I wanted her to open up. I realized I couldn't reverse the past, but I could address the present. As she tearfully expressed the pain of a grieving heart, I actually grieved with her even though I was the cause of much of that pain. Tears streamed down my cheeks as I embraced the woman I had hurt.

Then it happened. A presence seemed to fill the room—a supernatural presence. It was as if God the Holy Spirit entered the room and enveloped my arms with his to embrace Barbara too. He was there, as the comforting and healing God.

. . .

As Steve truly listened to how I (Barbara) was feeling, as we wept together, and as we sensed God weeping with us—something took place within me. The thick protective walls that kept me from feeling Steve's love and devotion were being penetrated. It didn't all happen overnight, but brick by brick, the prison in which I lived was coming down. I was beginning to feel accepted and safe. The fear that had paralyzed my life was being expelled. It was just as Scripture states: a Godlike "love has no fear, because perfect love expels all fear" (1 John 4:18).

 Pause and imagine how God showing up in a fresh way in your marriage would change things.

Walk in the light while you can, so the darkness will not overtake you.

JOHN 12:35

The darkness of foolishness is always chasing you. If you stop walking in God's light, the outcome is certain. Darkness will consume or overtake you. Our hope is in the light, and his name is Jesus!

Pray a brief prayer asking Jesus to keep you from the darkness and to empower you to walk in his light.

Lord, keep me from the darkness and the pain of my own foolishness. Give me the power to walk in your light. I especially need you to . . .

♥ Claim the promise of Psalm 43:3 — "Send out your light and your truth; let them guide me. Let them lead me to your holy mountain, to the place where you live."

DAY 26

Life as a Prodigal

Making It Personal

"And while he was still a long way off, his father saw him coming. Filled with love and compassion, he ran to his son, embraced him, and kissed him."

LUKE 15:20

Jesus told the parable of a father who had two sons (Luke 15:11–31). The younger son asked for his share of the family inheritance and was so self-centered that he couldn't wait for the father's death to receive his portion of the estate. After receiving his inheritance, the younger son traveled to a distant country and wasted all his money on extravagant living. We call this son, "the prodigal."

The prodigal son became so destitute that he was forced to work, feeding and caring for farm animals. When he reached the point of envying the food that the pigs were eating, the young son came to his senses and headed home.

Upon his return home, the prodigal had every intention of begging his father to make him one of the hired servants because he expected his relationship with his father to be severed and beyond repair. While the son was still far away, his father saw him and was moved with compassion. The father ran toward his son, fell into the young man's arms, kissed him, welcomed him, and celebrated his return.

Reflect on this parable and any ways you might relate to the prodigal.

My Personal Story

We have all lived various aspects of the prodigal story.

We've each lived parts of our lives with some amount of these three hindrances to intimacy.

- Selfishness
- Self-Reliance
- Self-Condemnation

We've also lived parts of our lives with some of the same struggles that the prodigal endured. We have:

- Exercised poor judgment
- Squandered or wasted precious things, opportunities, or relationships

Selfishness There have been times when you prioritized your own needs at the expense of others. All of us, at times, have acted selfishly or demanded that we get our way, saying, "Give me what's mine."	Have there been times when you have insisted on your own way, demanded your rights, or thought more highly of yourself and your agenda than your spouse? *Sadly at times, I* _____ _____ _____ _____ .
Self-Reliance There have been times when you have insisted on going it alone, denying you have needs, taking matters into your own hands, just like the prodigal. "I got myself into this mess, I'll get myself out."	Have there been times when you have lived life with pride, wanted to go it alone, had an attitude of not needing your partner, or denied that you even had needs? *Sadly at times, I* _____ _____ _____ _____ .
Self-Condemnation There have been times when you have questioned your own worth, struggled to share your needs, or considered yourself not important enough to have them met, saying, "I'm not worthy."	Have there been times when you have been reluctant to share your needs because you weren't sure you were worth having them met or reasoned that you are somehow not important? *Sadly at times, I* _____ _____ _____ _____ .

Poor Judgment	Have there been times when you've gone to places (either real or online) that you later regret or found yourself in circumstances that were harmful to you or your relationships? *Sadly at times, I* _____ _____ _____ _____ _____.
There have been times when you've gone to places (even to places on the internet) you should not have been. You've been in circumstances where you've lost your senses or made choices that you deeply regret.	
Squandering Precious Things	Have there been moments of wasted time, opportunities, or relationships for you? Any misplaced priorities? *Sadly at times, I* _____ _____ _____.
Each of us, at times, has squandered, misused, or wasted time, opportunities, or relationships.	

Pause and ask God to bring to mind any of the ways you might, at times, live like the prodigal. Quietly acknowledge these things with the Lord in prayer. Be confident though, because our heavenly Father has not left us without instruction. He welcomes you back home, just as he did the prodigal. Remember how God has given his Word and his promise to set us free (Romans 8:32).

God, I am saddened as I consider how I . . .

Please forgive me and change me. Thank you for doing so. I'm grateful for your grace because . . .

L10. A Spirit-empowered disciple becomes more and more like Jesus by imitating him and enjoying consistent times of being in his presence.

Just like the Fergusons and the Uhlmanns, each one of us has hurt our spouse. The hurts have come in many different ways because we are imperfect people who are married to imperfect people. Because we're human, we will inevitably hurt one another. Just because you are human, there have been times when you have hurt your partner, and, unintentionally, you have even hurt God. But have you truly healed those hurts? Let's begin that process now.

Take some time *alone* with the Lord. Circle some of the ways in which you may have hurt your spouse, your marriage, and the Lord. Consider this: *Have there been times when I was . . .*

selfish	unaccepting
critical	not dependable
negative	untrustworthy
insensitive	mean-spirited
disrespectful	belittling
verbally abusive	humiliating
unsupportive	embarrassing to my spouse
ungrateful	dismissive
unfaithful	inattentive
rejecting	unloving
unforgiving	living out wrong priorities
arrogant	harsh with my words or my tone
prideful	judgmental
manipulative	emotionally cold or distant

Scripture tells us that, "If we confess our sins to him, he can be depended on to forgive us and to cleanse us from every wrong" (1 John 1:9). God longs to hear your confession so you can experience his loving forgiveness.

Here's an example of what your confession to God might sound like. Do this Bible verse by writing your own confession to God in prayer.

God, I have deeply hurt you and my spouse by my . . .

These things were very wrong of me. I ask you to forgive me for how I have hurt you, my marriage and my spouse. I'm asking you to change me in these ways . . .

Thank you for your forgiveness.

W7. A Spirit-empowered disciple consistently looks for new ways that God's Word can be lived out in life—looking for ways Scripture can bring transformation in ongoing ways.

My Marriage Story

If we confess our sins to him, he can be depended on to forgive us and cleanse us from every wrong.

1 JOHN 1:9

First John 1:9 is the verse that we need to experience when we address the ways we have hurt God.

James 5:16 is the Scripture we need to experience when we have hurt someone else.

Confess your sins to each other and pray for each other so that you may be healed.

JAMES 5:16

You will learn how to do this Bible verse and live it out during your Marriage Staff Meeting on Day 28.

Lessons from the Compassionate Father

My Jesus Story

*"But his father said to the servants,
'Quick! Bring the finest robe in the house and put it on him.
Get a ring for his finger and sandals for his feet . . .
We must celebrate . . . "*

LUKE 15:22–23

Let's reflect again on the story of the prodigal son, but this time we'll focus more on the father. As you reread the story of the prodigal and his father, allow the Lord to sensitize your heart to the real God. Spend some time meditating on this passage of Scripture. Ponder not only the story itself but also the ways in which the heart of the heavenly Father is revealed through the story.

Allow the Lord to show his heart of love and compassion *for you*!

His Story

The story of the prodigal son gives us a picture of the true heart of God. The most gripping scene in this biblical account finds the father waiting for his wayward son. He scans the horizon day after day, straining his eyes and hoping to catch a glimpse of his son—the young man who demanded an early inheritance, ran away from home, and squandered every cent his father had so graciously given.

Before you reread the story, take a moment to reflect again on the things you have in common with the prodigal.

- Like the prodigal, have there been times when you have made selfish demands? This could have been preoccupation with your own agenda or as overt as manipulation or control.

- Like the prodigal, has your own self-reliance ever led you to foolishly conclude that you could "take care of things yourself"? Have you ever minimized your need for God or other people because of a mistaken conclusion that you are better off on your own?

- The wayward son also discounted his own worth to the Father. Have you ever questioned your worth to your heavenly Father, thus allowing self-condemnation to rob you of joy and passion for the Lord?

- Have you, like the prodigal, fallen victim to a lifestyle of poor choices and pain-filled consequences?

- Have you been in places that you should not have been?

- Have you been insensitive toward those you love rather than giving them honor or made choices about life that you regret?

- Have you squandered precious things: wasted moments of special time, relationships, or opportunities?

- Have there been misplaced priorities or regrets about what could have been?

Now spend some time meditating on the prodigal story from Scripture. Read Luke 15:11–31 and focus on what this passage tells you about the character of your heavenly Father. Allow the Holy Spirit to sensitize your heart to the true character of God.

Picture the young man who has selfishly taken from his father and wasted all he was given. He self-reliantly takes matters into his own hands and from the pigpen questions his worth to the Father. Only when he finds himself feeding pigs does the son come to his senses. The prodigal turns from his choices and decides to go home. Picture him walking along dusty, winding roads. He turns the last corner toward home and catches a glimpse of his father running towards him in the distance.

Allow the Holy Spirit to lead you into a fresh experience of God's love: "And while he was still a long way off, his father saw him coming. Filled with love and compassion, he ran to his son, embraced him and kissed him" (Luke 15:20).

Jesus is compassionate towards you and wants to restore relationship with you.
Luke 15:20

Your Jesus Story

Put yourself into the story. Imagine that the Father is waiting for you to return home. When he sees you in the distance, he is moved with compassion. In spite of your selfishness, self-reliance, self-condemnation, wrong choices, and sin, the Father can't wait to share his love with you. He leaps quickly and anxiously off the front porch because he cannot wait to see you. Your Father hugs you, kisses you, and whispers in your ear. He doesn't offer lectures or criticism. There is no rebuke or scorn. His voice is filled with compassion as he embraces you. There is a ring, a robe, and the announcement of a party. Your Father welcomes you with outstretched arms, thrilled to embrace you and excited to love you!

Let God fill your heart with thanksgiving for the grace that you have received. Ask him to bring you back often to this time when you encountered the love of the Father. Pray that God would fill you with wonder and gratitude.

Heavenly Father, I am grateful for your forgiveness. I'm grateful that you love and forgive me. Thank you that you are . . .

L3. A Spirit-empowered disciple develops a correct view of God as the Lord reveals himself; enjoying more and more closeness with him.

DAY 28

Sharing Your Week 4 Journey

He leads the humble in doing right, teaching them his way.

PSALM 25:9

Marriage Staff Meeting

The following experiential exercises are practical demonstrations of how to acknowledge your imperfections and need for growth. These exercises also serve as a practical demonstration of accountability to God and to your spouse.

Share Your Personal Story

Reflect on your work from the previous day's readings and be prepared to share them with your partner.

Embrace gratitude for God's forgiveness. Share these words with one another.

 I have claimed 1 John 1:9 and confessed to God the ways in which I have hurt you and our marriage. I'm grateful because the Father has forgiven me and restored me. My experience with God was meaningful because . . .

Embrace the truth.

There's nothing that you could do to earn the gift of God's Son. Every one of us must conclude: it's only by his grace. It is only God's unconditional love that provided the gift of Calvary and the forgiveness that is available to us. Allow the Holy Spirit to touch your heart with praise and gratitude that God has freely given the gift of his Son. His forgiveness for you is guaranteed because of Calvary.

Take the next few moments to reflect on what you have done or could do to deserve God's forgiveness. Embrace God's truth together and then share a few moments of prayer with your spouse. Pray silently or out loud.

> *God, when I consider the undeserved gift of your Son and your unfailing love and complete and constant forgiveness just for me, my heart is touched with . . .*

Next, pray silently or aloud. Tell the Lord that you are willing to be a good steward of his forgiveness—one who faithfully forgives others as you have been forgiven. Tell him that you are ready to let go of anger and ask his Spirit to empower more reconciliation and peace for your marriage.

> *God, because you have forgiven me, I want to be forgiving to my spouse. I'm ready to let go of any anger I might have. I'm asking your Spirit to bring more reconciliation, peace, and forgiveness to our marriage. I am ready to do my part.*

SPIRIT EMPOWERED Faith P8. A Spirit-empowered disciple lives in peaceful relationships and works to help others live in God's peace as well.

Share Your Marriage Stories

During this Marriage Staff Meeting, you and your spouse will experience several distinct Bible verses.

Doing the Bible

Confess your sins to each other and pray
for each other so that you may be healed.

JAMES 5:16

Take the next moments to share your confessions with your partner, request forgiveness, and pray for God to heal the hurt. It is important to use the following outline as you share your confession. Here's an example of what your confession to your spouse might sound like. Use the sentence prompts just as they are given below. (For example: "wrong" is much better to say than "sorry" since to confess means "to agree with God," and God has said these things are wrong.)

Be specific: *I've seen how I have hurt you deeply by* _____
_____.

Demonstrate understanding: *I know you must have felt* _____
_____.

Admit wrong: *It was wrong of me to* _____
_____.

Request Forgiveness: *Will you forgive me?*_____
_____.

- When your spouse asks for forgiveness, remember: forgiveness is a choice, not primarily a feeling. The question is not "Do you feel like forgiving?" but "Will you?" Will you release or drop the offense? As you make this choice to forgive, new feelings will come.

- When your spouse asks for forgiveness, remember: forgiveness is an issue of stewardship. It is really *God's* forgiveness that you have received and are now being asked to share with your spouse. Just as God has forgiven you, you are called to love the same.

As you express forgiveness for one another, you will be *doing* the Bible.

Get rid of all bitterness, rage, anger, harsh words, and slander, as well as all types of evil behavior. Instead, be kind to each other, tenderhearted, forgiving one another, just as God through Christ has forgiven you.

EPHESIANS 4:31–32

After all needed confessions have been shared, pray for your spouse. Ask God to heal your partner's hurt.

God, please heal my husband's/wife's hurt. I know he/she is hurting because of my _____ and my _____. Lord, please heal his/her heart and change me.

Repeat the confession process above as many times as needed. Claim this promise of healing as you do his Book: "Confess your sins to each other and pray for each other so that you may be healed" (James 5:16).

Practical Suggestions for Your Times of Confession:

After each person has shared his or her points of confession, it can also be important to ask:

"Are there any other significant hurts that need my confession? Please share them with me so I can apologize and ask your forgiveness."

This question allows your spouse to share hurts you may not be aware of but still need your confession. Use the same confession outline above to respond to what your partner shares.

Finally, there are times when it may also be important to gain a deeper understanding of your partner's hurt. Further understanding the dimensions of your partner's pain strengthens the healing in your relationship. It's in these times you will want to offer comfort and confession. Here are some helpful hints for this kind of conversation.

- Set aside an unhurried amount of time and provide a safe place for your spouse to talk. Offer to listen to any of the hurt that your partner would like to share and be ready to give words of comfort and compassion—then confession as needed. Here's what it might sound like to begin this conversation.

I have a renewed desire to bring healing to the ways I have hurt you. I know that I have hurt you by . . .

I want to really understand your pain, so I would like for you to take as long as you need to share with me how I have hurt you. I want to know how you feel.

- Give your spouse plenty of time to share hurts that need to be addressed.

    As your spouse is sharing, allow the Comforter to move your heart with compassion. When it's time to respond, say words that are filled with tenderness, such as:

    I'm so sad that I hurt you in these ways.

    I deeply regret how painful my actions were for you.

    I now understand more about the pain I caused. I can understand how you would feel . . .

    I can see how I was wrong to . . . (share more confessions as needed). Will you forgive me?

    I am praying that God will remind me of the hurt you've felt, that he will change me, and that you will come to trust me not to hurt you in these ways again.

    You and your partner will experience the blessing of living one more Bible verse. You'll be doing Romans 12:15 and James 5:16.

    Weep with those who weep.

    ROMANS 12:15

Share Your Reflections from Your Jesus Stories

Imagine Jesus running off the front porch as he did for the prodigal. Remember that Jesus welcomes you and celebrates you!

When I imagine the picture of Jesus running to me, embracing me with words of compassion, and celebrating over me, I . . .

As a final exercise with your partner, take some time to pray together. Pray a special kind of prayer: a "perfect love" prayer. In the moments of your prayer time, allow some of God's perfect love he has placed in you to begin to cast out a measure of your spouse's fear.

Doing the Bible

Before you begin your prayer, remember the list of the Top Ten Relational Needs. Given the confession that you shared and the conversations you've had recently with your spouse, how might God want you to change? Might he want you to become more:

- Accepting
- Affectionate
- Attentive
- Appreciative
- Approving

- Compassionate
- Encouraging
- Respectful
- Supportive
- Secure-giving

There is no fear in love; but perfect love casts out fear.

1 JOHN 4:18 NASB

After you've quietly reflected and heard from the Lord, begin praying with your spouse.

Pray out loud and allow your spouse (and possibly your small group) to overhear your prayer. Allow God's perfect love to push out your partner's fear. Allow God's reassuring love to give your spouse more freedom to trust that God will bring about the changes you've identified. We call this kind of praying "Perfect Love Praying." Your prayer might sound like this:

God, I am asking you to change me and make me more (attentive, supportive, respectful, etc) . . .

I want you to make these changes in me because I love _____ *and I want to love him/her in even more meaningful ways.*

♥ Claim the promise of 1 John 5:14–15. You are praying according to his will. You are asking God to change you so that you are more like him. You can be confident that he hears you, and you will have the request that you ask!

 W7. A Spirit-empowerd disciple consistently looks for new ways that God's Word can be lived out—looking for ways it can bring transformation in ongoing ways.

CALLED 2 LOVE MEANS:

- Confessing your wrongs to God and to your partner and asking for forgiveness.

- Forgiving your partner as God has forgiven you.

- Seeking to understand your spouse's pain and sharing words of compassion.

- Praying for God to change you and heal your partner's hurt.

MARRIAGE INTIMACY IS DEEPENED AS YOU CONTINUE DOING THE BIBLE AND EXPERIENCING:

- Ephesians 4:31–32—forgiving one another as we have been forgiven by Christ.

- 1 John 1:9—confessing your sins to God.

- James 5:16—confessing your sins to one another.

- Ephesians 4:31–32—forgiving one another.

- Romans 12:15b—mourning as your partner mourns.

- 1 John 4:18—continuing to pray for God to change you and remove your partner's fear.

YOUR RELATIONSHIP WITH JESUS IS DEEPENED AS YOU:

- Imagine Jesus embracing you and celebrating over you in spite of your wrong choices.

- Imagine Jesus crying for you because he sees the ways you are hurt and is moved with compassion.

- Imagine Jesus forgiving and empowering you to share his forgiveness with others.

Who Will Deliver Me?

*I want to do what is good, but I don't. I don't want to do what is wrong, but I do it anyway
. . . Oh, what a miserable person I am! Who will free me from this life that is dominated
by sin and death? Thank God! The answer is in Jesus Christ our Lord.*

ROMANS 7:19, 24–25

Admit it. Throughout our lives, we all struggle occasionally to make true change happen. At times, we've made empty and unfulfilled promises to act differently. These broken promises can produce frustration, confusion, and discouragement in marriage.

Our hope for lasting transformation doesn't rely on new promises, careful plans, or recommitments. Our hope for change is in a Person! Jesus and the promise of his Spirit's work in us bring the freedom, adequacy, and motivation to genuinely change.

As you read the Uhlmann's next story, be encouraged as their journey into marriage intimacy gains momentum.

Becoming A.W.A.R.E

I (Steve) was among those who hated to be wrong. If anyone suggested I was wrong, I either got defensive or avoided discussing the subject altogether. Because Barbara rarely resisted or disagreed with me, everything went along smoothly on the outside. All the while, the inner tension, fear, and pain ate away inside her, until it emerged with her panic attacks.

Being human, we are all naturally inclined to defend and justify ourselves. That inclination works against experiencing and maintaining an intimate connection with another.

My self-centeredness and self-defense mechanisms only encouraged Barbara to remain closed. Only when I was willing to stop pointing my finger at her and take full responsibility for my actions did she start to feel safe enough to open up and speak out.

The change in me didn't happen quickly. It was a process. I learned to be aware of some key steps to help me through the process. Barbara and I both locked onto a process we call AWARE. That's an acronym for the relationship discovery process in pursuit of knowing and loving each other and becoming more relationally intimate. It has been working for both of us. Here's what we did and still do:

Acknowledge we have issues and areas for growth then place ourselves in accountability to each other and to the Lord.

Work with our story of brokenness to better understand why we do what we do.

Agree with God about our condition and turn to him as the change agent.

Rely on the Holy Spirit to love each other as Jesus loves.

Empower change as we develop new habits and patterns of behavior.

Aware:

I ACKNOWLEDGE that I have issues and areas for growth then place myself in accountability to my spouse (near one) and to the Lord.

In my desire to love more like Jesus, I started by sitting down on Sunday afternoons and reviewing my week relative to my awareness of loving Barbara.

I would read the definition of love from 1 Corinthians 13:4–6 and personalize it by substituting my name when the word love was used. I would then think of the past week and recall whether:

- Steve was patient.
- Steve was kind.
- Steve was not jealous or boastful or proud or rude.
- Steve did not demand his own way.
- Steve was not irritable, and he kept no record of being wronged.
- Steve did not rejoice about injustice but rejoiced whenever the truth won out.

I was acknowledging each week that I needed the Holy Spirit in order to love like Jesus. I was becoming aware that I couldn't do it on my own. I not only needed God, but I needed Barbara as well. I needed her to hold me in loving account too. She knew my struggles and weaknesses and I needed her to help me evaluate and measure how I was doing.

I actually asked Barbara to rate me on a scale of 1 to 10 regarding the characteristics of love from 1 Corinthians 13. About every six weeks, I would ask, "How am I doing on being patient and kind? How am I doing on not demanding my own way? How am I doing on not being irritable, etc.?"

I admit I didn't get high scores when we first started. Neither did Barbara. After rating each other, we'd ask how we could do better. Over time, we both became sensitive to the relational needs each of us had and literally began to meet them.

aWare:

We WORK with our story of brokenness to better understand why we do what we do.

How did I (Steve) become a workaholic? Why do I always feel I have to be in control of things? Why do I tend to be so self-centered and think things have to go my way?

How did I (Barbara) become such a people pleaser? Why do I avoid conflict like the plague? Why do I tend to feel so unworthy and keep people from getting too close to me emotionally?

Those questions are naturally uncomfortable because they indicate we have growth areas in our lives. No one is ever perfect except one, and he (Jesus) was God incarnate. For the rest of us, it's just a matter of varying degrees of brokenness. If we don't acknowledge our need to grow in Christlikeness and work with our story of brokenness, we become our own worst enemy.

As soon as Barbara and I were able to accept the truth of our imperfections and began to understand our story of brokenness, we were on our way to recovery. We learned that exploring our brokenness includes both embracing our need to grow in Christlikeness as well as taking a careful look at how our growing up experiences have impacted our current relationships. We are imperfect people who have grown up around other imperfect people, which leads to less than perfect results.

Understanding our top relational needs and respective stories of brokenness was crucial to our healing. It began to help us make sense of why Steve was a workaholic and set on control and why Barbara couldn't feel emotionally or let anyone in.

The better we understood our story of brokenness, the better we connected the dots of why we were doing the things we did. The longer we neglected the emotional buildup of unhealed pain, the worse we got. That reality was powerfully driven home by a greater understanding of the Emotional Cup in our lives.

Understanding our story of brokenness and why we were doing what we were doing was incredibly helpful. However, the change we were desiring wouldn't just happen from realizing where our issues and brokenness originated and from whom. A willingness to change and the power to make that change were needed.

 Pause and envision both you and your spouse humbly embracing a commitment to a deepened work of Christ-likeness. Your marriage is worth it!

Spend the next few moments in prayer. Talk to God about giving you more:

FREEDOM from your powerless efforts to change or improve your life. Tell God that you are choosing Jesus instead of a tendency to justify, rationalize, and blame.

ADEQUACY to change. Tell God that you yield to the One who *is* love and want God's Spirit to empower you to truly love like Jesus.

MOTIVATION to change. Tell God about your overwhelming gratitude for how you have first been loved.

Pray a prayer like the one below:

You have loved me with a 1 Corinthians 13 kind of love. Show me how well I'm doing at loving my spouse in these same ways. Have I . . .

- *been patient?*

- *been kind?*

- *been jealous, boastful, prideful, or rude?*

- *demanded my own way?*

- *been irritable or kept a record of being wronged?*

- *rejoiced in injustice or when the truth won out?*

I yield to your Spirit and ask you to change me and love others through me.

♥ Claim the promise of Romans 5:5 — "And this hope will not lead to disappointment. For we know how dearly God loves us, because he has given us the Holy Spirit to fill our hearts with his love."

Yes, each of us will give a personal account to God.

ROMANS 14:12

God Knows How!

*So all of us who have had that veil removed can see and
reflect the glory of the Lord. And the Lord—who is the Spirit—
makes us more and more like him as we are changed
into his glorious image.*

2 CORINTHIANS 3:18

The truth is this: we have little or no hope of lasting change on our own. Only Jesus knows how to bring about all the changes we desire. On our own, we lack the insight, motivation, and power to love like Jesus. But guess what? Jesus knows this too.

The best news is that Christ has given us his Spirit to be ever-present and available to change us into the likeness of Jesus. This progressive and on-going transformation identifies us as his followers and empowers our deepened intimacy in marriage.

As you read the Uhlmann's story, remember to celebrate some of the changes in attitudes, actions, and priorities that you've experienced in this *Called 2 Love* journey.

Continuing to Become A.W.A.R.E.

awAre:

We AGREE with God about our condition and turn to him as the Change Agent.

In my research about change, I (Steve) ran across the word "plasticity." The meaning in context of neuroscience describes the ability of the brain to be molded into new ways of responding. Our brains can literally form new neuro-pathways. This confirms what Scripture has promised for the believer's journey in Christlikeness (see 2 Corinthians 5:17).

Neuroscientists have confirmed that the human brain, even when fully mature, is far more plastic—changing and malleable—than we originally thought. Essentially, the brain (at all ages) is highly responsive to stimuli, and connections between neurons are dynamic and can rapidly change within minutes of stimulation. Our experiences of Scripture, encounters with Jesus, and engagement in caring community provide just the right "stimuli" for this transformation.

I (Steve) can tell you that Barbara is a changed woman after her bout with cancer, panic attacks, and PTSD. Because of her encounters with God, Barbara has become vulnerable and has learned to express much of what she feels. Her brain is being reprogrammed through deepened intimacy with the Lord and in our marriage.

I (Barbara) can tell you that Steve is a changed man. He has become more tender and kind, shows attention to me, and has become a good listener. His priorities have changed, and he is no longer such a driven man. Steve's brain is being reprogrammed as the Holy Spirit empowers him to experience Scripture and encounter more and more moments with Jesus.

The change we have experienced has brought us to a point of enjoying each other, wanting to always be with each other, and finding life to be so full of meaning and purpose in just loving one another. What a change in us and our home!

"And the Lord—who is the Spirit—makes us more and more like him as we change into his glorious image" (2 Corinthians 3:18).

awaRe:

We RELY on the Holy Spirit to love like Jesus loves.

As Barbara and I evaluate our journey towards greater intimacy, it's not so much about what we've learned over these past years as it is about "learning how to re-learn." Relational and spiritual growth isn't a formula or a list of 5 or 12 steps we've taken that has changed our lives. It's been a journey of re-learning how to discover God and one another.

Something struck me as I (Steve) read verses like: "Jesus has the power of God, by which he has given us everything we need to live and to serve God. We have these things because we know him. Jesus called us by his glory and goodness" (2 Peter 1:3 NCV), and "You are living a brand new kind of life that is continually learning more and more of what is right, and trying constantly to be more and more like Christ who created this new life within you" (Colossians 3:10 TLB). It seemed that knowing Jesus better and learning more about him was directly linked to being and loving like him. I began thinking of the Holy Spirit as my daily coach. He was the One who would be with me everyday. He was the One I could come to know, and he was the One who would give me direction and guidance.

To this day, I wake up with: *Coach, what are we going to change today?* Starting my day looking for change puts me in a receptive mindset for the Holy Spirit to bring about a Christlike transformation in my life.

When we rely on the Holy Spirit (our Coach), he *"produces this kind of fruit in our lives: love, joy, peace, patience, kindness, goodness, faithfulness, gentleness, and self-control"* (Galatians 5:22–23).

awarE:

We EMPOWER change as we develop new habits and patterns of behavior.

This pattern for success was making a real difference. A transformation was taking place. New habits were being programmed into both of us to replace the old, unconscious, learned behavior. Steve and I both were realizing something supernatural was taking place.

Marriage intimacy and life transformation doesn't happen when we focus solely on the rational and behavioral. Just knowing, learning, or memorizing principles (even biblical principles) doesn't necessarily bring about change. Likewise, knowing how to behave and white-knuckling your way into life transformation isn't sustainable either. The rational and behavioral models for change call on us to know and do but are rooted in our ability—not the Holy Spirit.

What's missing is the need to experience the presence and power of the living God. If we want true change and transformation in our marriage, we must exchange a rational and behavioral model of transformation for a relational and experiential one. Our hope for change is in Jesus! Our relational connection to Jesus is what produces Christ-likeness.

What's missing is the absolute imperative of a relational model that calls us not only to know God's truth but also to be empowered to experience it. Our hope for change is in fresh encounters with Jesus and frequent experiences of his Word lived out in true community with others.

(See Appendices 3–4. These provide additional insights about this relational purpose of truth.)

Pause and imagine the possibilities and potentials of intimacy in marriage as you expect your Coach to bring about more and more Christlikeness.

"Students are not greater than their teacher.
But the student who is fully trained will become like the teacher."

LUKE 6:40

We can celebrate that we have a Teacher who can lead us in living and loving like Jesus. As we practice being in the presence of the Lord, we will become like him!

♥ Take a moment to listen to what the Holy Spirit might be saying and claim the truths of 1 John 2:27:

But you have received the Holy Spirit, and he lives within you,
so you don't need anyone to teach you what is true. For the Spirit teaches you
everything you need to know, and what he teaches is true—it is not a lie.
So just as he has taught you, remain in fellowship with Christ.

Notice that last key phrase "remain in fellowship with Christ." It is important. For real change to affect each area of our lives and marriages, we must consistently invite the Holy Spirit to do his work in us, and we must remain sensitive to listen and respond to his teaching. Declare that willingness now.

Thank you Holy Spirit, for leading me and teaching me to be more and more like
Jesus. I yield to you in my life and marriage. I want to hear you, yield to you, and live in
response to your Word. I specifically want to remain in your fellowship as I . . .

WEEK FIVE

Attentive, Intentional, and Need-Focused

*Jesus realized at once that healing power had gone out from him,
so he turned around in the crowd and asked, "Who touched my robe?"*

MARK 5:30

The marriage intimacy journey requires us to love like Jesus. That requires supernatural strength. On our own, maintaining closeness and intimacy in marriage is next to impossible. Therefore, what does loving like Jesus actually look like?

We don't have to look too far into the Gospels to see how Jesus loved. He was:

- ATTENTIVE—He noticed people's need.

- INTENTIONAL—He carried out specific actions and plans.

- NEED-FOCUSED—Jesus prioritized giving to others.

As you read this next part of the Uhlmann's story, we will focus on the priority of giving all of yourself—spirit, soul, and body to your spouse. Celebrate the truth that you have the opportunity to become more attentive, intentional, and need-focused, even in your sexual intimacy.

WEEK FIVE

The Gift of Sexual Intimacy

In every marriage course like this one, there are one or two obligatory chapters on sex. It's just one of those topics you must cover. But why? Here is the pragmatic answer: sexual issues are always among the top reasons for marital conflict and even divorce. Many couples fight about sex, and they don't know where to go for answers. In addition to the marriages that dissolve because of sexual infidelity, many more couples endure decades of sexual disappointment. We (Steve and Barbara) were one of those couples. Although sex was a regular part of our marriage, it felt more like an obligation that Barbara owed to Steve.

One of the most profound game-changers in our marriage has been to recognize that a "so-so" sex life is not God's plan for any marriage. God cares about your sexual relationship.

First Corinthians 7:3–5 is often used to justify the importance of sex in a Christian marriage. Here is what Paul writes:

> The husband should fulfill his wife's sexual needs, and the wife should fulfill her husband's needs. The wife gives authority over her body to her husband, and the husband gives authority over his body to his wife. Do not deprive each other of sexual relations, unless you both agree to refrain from sexual intimacy for a limited time so you can give yourselves more completely to prayer. Afterward, you should come together again so that Satan won't be able to tempt you because of your lack of self-control.

At first glance, this passage seems to simply say "you owe each other regular sex because you will be tempted to stray if you neglect your sex life." But what Paul is actually saying in context with other passages on marriage is far more profound. Sexual intimacy between a Christian husband and wife is to be viewed as a mutual gift exchange. It is a profound way that a man and a woman say with their bodies, "I give myself completely to you." In sexual intimacy, husband and wife engage in a physical celebration with their bodies, marking the covenant they have made to one another. Some theologians, such as Timothy Keller, describe sexual intimacy as a sacrament: a physical way that we remember a spiritual truth. This is why God created sex to be holy, vulnerable, pleasurable, and frequent within marriage.

Unfortunately, the experience for many married couples doesn't approximate what God intended. Instead, sex often represents feelings of resentment and fear.

You don't have to look very far to see that sex is messed up in our culture. All around us are evidences of how God's beautiful design for sex has been vandalized. Satan distorts sexuality by tempting us to separate the spiritual and relational significance of our sexuality. Pornography, hookups, and prostitution are obvious examples of this destruction. Yet, we often don't realize that a Christian marriage is the most powerful place to reclaim all that God created sex to be. Marital intimacy is the one place where we get to play "offense" in a spiritual battle where we so often feel defeated by counterfeits.

When Christian couples settle for subpar intimacy, they give up a tremendous opportunity to honor God within marriage. Most couples don't just decide to "not like sex," but they settle because they are confused about how to take steps toward health and wholeness.

A great place to start working on your sex life is to prayerfully ask yourself and your spouse, "How have we allowed satan to rob us of God's best in the area of our sexuality?"

Pause and reflect on how you might be more attentive, intentional, and need-focused with your spouse—even in your sexual intimacy.

Oh, how beautiful you are!
How pleasing, my love, how full of delights!

SONG OF SOLOMON 7:6

Many Christian couples feel strange about inviting God into their sex lives. News flash: God created you as a sexual person. He inspired Solomon to write an erotic poem about marital sexual love to be included in our Holy Scriptures. He created sexual intimacy as a gift for you.

Have you ever prayed together about your sex life? If not, try it! Take some time together right now to ask God to help you honor him and one another in this important and special area of your marriage.

Thank you, Father, for the gift of sexuality and the physical intimacy we can enjoy in marriage. We want to honor you and one another in this area of our relationship, so show us how to celebrate this gift

♥ Claim the promise of Jeremiah 33:3 — *"Ask me and I will tell you remarkable secrets you do not know about things to come."*

WEEK FIVE

DAY 32

When God Shows Up, Good Things Happen!

Oh, that you would burst from the heavens and come down!
How the mountains would quake in your presence!

ISAIAH 64:1

When God shows up, he changes everything for the better.

We pray that you and your spouse have seen God show up along this *Called 2 Love* journey. It's important to stop and celebrate these God-encounters and the important changes that the Holy Spirit brings. Pausing to celebrate what God has done gives us hope for more. More encounters with Jesus means more Christlikeness in us. More Christlikeness in us results in more intimacy in our marriage!

As you read this following encouragement from the Uhlmanns, remember that God wants abundance and good things in every part of your relationship—including your physical intimacy. Read the Uhlmann's perspective and then practice your sexual intimacy!

WEEK FIVE

The Difference between Sexual Activity and Sexual Intimacy

Our (Steve and Barbara) mutual friend, Dr. Juli Slattery, author of *Rethinking Sexuality: God's Design and Why It Matters*, explains the difference between sexual activity and sexual intimacy.

It is normal to experience obstacles in your sex life. A history of pornography. Differing levels of desire. Pain during intercourse. Inability to "sexually perform" or experience orgasm. Arguments about when and how often to have sex. Fatigue, depression, and illnesses that sap desire. Triggers from past trauma that make sex feel unsafe. These are just some of the hurdles that Christian married couples are likely to confront throughout a lifetime of sex together. It's enough to make many people ask God, *Why did you create sex in the first place?* It seems to cause more conflict than unity and more pain than pleasure.

While everyone wishes for an uncomplicated and naturally fulfilling sex life, it could be that the obstacles themselves are part of the journey of marital intimacy.

Most of us enter marriage defining a great sex life by measure of sexual *activity*. We think of sex being good when it is based on flawless bodies, compatibility, and frequent mutual pleasure. When those things don't naturally happen, we think that the "gift" of sex is broken.

Instead of focusing on these measures of sexual activity, God would rather direct our attention to building sexual *intimacy*. What's the difference? Sexual intimacy is a journey, not an event. The focus is on who you are becoming as a married couple not just on how satisfying a sexual experience might be in the moment.

Sex is an expression of love (see Ephesians 5), but it is also a great test of love. Husbands, will you love your wife as Christ loves the church? Sacrificing even your own body to prize her and make her holy? Wives, will you honor your husband and nurture his masculinity? Together, will you learn to love each other exclusively, sacrificially, and passionately?

You see, you can view every obstacle you have encountered in the bedroom as an invitation to love. A long-term, fulfilling sex life is absolutely impossible if both of you are unwilling to learn to love as Christ Jesus loves us. Forgiveness, mercy, grace, unselfishness, speaking the truth in love . . . these are the character traits that God desires to develop in all of his children. "Since God chose you to be the holy people he loves, you must clothe yourselves with tenderhearted mercy, kindness, humility, gentleness and patience. Make allowance for each other's faults, and forgive .... Remember, the Lord forgave you, so you must forgive others" (Colossians 3:12–13). These are the markers of true love and authentic intimacy.

Because sexual intimacy requires listening, sharing vulnerably, forgiveness, and patience, working on your sex life is an invitation to grow in the character qualities that represent the deepest kinds of love. This is why a couple with wrinkled bodies who have been married fifty years can gaze into each other's eyes with a passion that overshadows that of their honeymoon. Through the journey, they have not just "made love" but have also become lovers.

Pause and reflect on how you might demonstrate more compassion, kindness, humility, gentleness, and patience with your spouse—some of the other true markers of intimacy.

What are some of the obstacles you and your spouse have encountered in your sexual relationship?

How could those obstacles become an invitation to learn to love?

Think about the current state of your sex life. Are you more focused on sexual *activity* or sexual *intimacy*? How would your conversations and sexual encounters change if the goal was truly to become sexually intimate?

Pray this prayer during your private moments with the Lord:

Lord, search my heart. I want every area of my life and marriage to reflect your character. Please help me to view the struggles we have in our sex life as invitations to learn to love as you would have me love. What do you want me to learn about love?

After you have heard from the Lord, share this with your spouse.

And finally, end this discussion by completing the Love Map exercise below. Let it be a part of a new expression of sexual intimacy with your partner.

♥ Claim the promise of John 15:11 — "I have told you these things so that you will be filled with my joy. Yes, your joy will overflow!"

DAY 33

Celebrate Deepened Marriage Intimacy

Making It Personal

And if someone asks about your hope as a believer,
always be ready to explain it.

1 PETER 3:15

As God continues to change you and your marriage, you will have a lot to celebrate! Transformation is good news. A changed life inspires hope.

First Peter tell us, if someone asks about our hope as a believer, we need to be ready to explain it. The hope we experience as believers and the change God brings to our lives is something to share. A part of the *Called 2 Love* journey is building upon your marriage story and cultivating your own testimony of hope so that you are ready to explain it to others.

Now's the time to begin journaling your story of hope.

My Personal Story

Take time now to reflect on your own *Called 2 Love* journey and the changes you have seen in your marriage and personal life.

- In what ways has God empowered that transformation?

- Are you more accepting, more forgiving, more comforting, or more respectful, patient, and kind as a result of God's love demonstrated through you?

- Are you less critical, less harsh, less angry, or less controlling as a result of God's love flowing through you?

Because of receiving God's love for me, I am now more . . .

Because of God's love for me, I am now less . . .

Celebrate these changes by giving credit where credit is due! Express your gratitude to the Lord.

God, I am grateful that you have made such a difference in my life by . . .

I will praise you, Lord, with all my heart;
I will tell of all the marvelous things you have done.

PSALM 9:1

 L1. A Spirit-empowered disciple consistently practices thanksgiving and gratitude for all things and in all circumstances.

Finally, consider how the Lord might want you to share with other people what he has done in you and in your marriage. First Thessalonians 2:8 reminds us that we are called to share the good news of Jesus with others. The Lord has done some amazing things in your life and in your marriage. You have some good news to share!

We loved you so much that we shared
with you not only God's Good News
but our own lives, too.

1 THESSALONIANS 2:8

God, who is it that might need to hear my story of how you have changed me and are transforming me? Show me, Lord. I am listening.

ASK GOD TO HELP YOU INITIATE CONVERSATIONS THAT ALLOW YOU TO:

Listen to someone's story.

You might even ask something like: "Hey, tell me how things are going in your relationship with _____ . What have you done for date night lately?"

Share your story.

Say something like: "There are times when I struggle with _____ in our marriage. But Jesus is making a difference in my life and my marriage by _____."

Then bridge to the Jesus story.

Say something like: "Let me tell you how I have seen Jesus enable me to _____ . I've experienced Jesus' unconditional love and acceptance in spite of my _____ and that's made things different in my life and in my marriage. Can I tell you more about him?"

 M8. A Spirit-empowered disciple actively engages in another's life story so that a personal story of transformation can be shared; tells how Jesus has made a difference in life.

DAY 34

Freedom from Condemnation

My Jesus Story

So Christ has truly set us free.
Now make sure that you stay free.

GALATIANS 5:1

Preparing your story of hope will reaffirm your God-given identity. Being ready to effectively share that hope with others will require a sure foundation of emotional health. We all need freedom from the painful emotions of hurt, anger, fear, guilt, and condemnation.

Read and reflect on the following exercises.

You will be reviewing the healing antidotes for each of these painful emotions and then focusing specifically on freedom from condemnation.

Your Jesus Story

Remember our earlier analogy of the brain and the cup from Day 19? Each of us has a part of our brain that's in charge of emotion. Just like a small cup, this part of our brain can only hold so much. When the emotional part of our brain is filled up with painful emotions, we experience certain symptoms that let us know our "emotional cup" is full.

It's also important to remember: experiencing painful emotions is inevitable. From our youngest days and now into our marriage, we are imperfect people who live around other imperfect people; therefore, it stands to reason—we will experience some amount of hurt.

Where does this hurt originate? Because we are imperfect people who live around others who are imperfect, our relational needs go UNMET at times. It's in these moments of unmet need when we experience HURT. If we don't know how to experience God's plans for healing our painful emotions, we hurt ALONE.

HURTING ALONE CAN PRODUCE:

- **Anger**, which is healed as we forgive.

- **Guilt** because of how we have acted. Guilt is healed through our confession.

- **Fear, anxiety, and worry** because we're afraid that more hurt is inevitable, unavoidable, and self-fulfilling. Fear is healed through reassuring love and meeting the need of security.

- **Condemnation or shame**, the sense that we somehow deserved to be hurt or we are just a bad person. Condemnation is healed by truthful reassurance concerning our worth and value.

As we reflect on the painful emotions that can fill our emotional cup, we celebrate that God has not left us without instruction. He gives us clear guidance about how to heal each emotion. Review the antidotes and Scripture verses that guide us in how to heal painful emotions.

HOW DO WE HEAL THESE PAINFUL EMOTIONS?

- **Comfort heals hurt** (Romans 12:15b, Matthew 5:4).

- **Confession heals guilt** (1 John 1:9; James 5:16).

- **God's perfect love removes fear** (1 John 4:18).

- **Forgiveness is the answer for our anger.** Ephesians 4:31–32 is our guide. As we choose to forgive as Christ has forgiven us, we can let go of anger and allow the peace of Christ to rule and reign in our relationships.

- The Bible tells us there is no condemnation in Christ Jesus (Romans 8:1)!

Therefore there is now no condemnation
for those who are in Christ Jesus.

ROMANS 8:1 NIV

So what do we do if we're experiencing condemnation? It is healed by embracing the truth of our God-given identity as his beloved. Embrace the truth that you are so special and important to him that Jesus is sitting at the right hand of the Father praying for you.

Who dares accuse us, whom God has chosen for his own?
No one—for God himself has given us right standing with himself.
Who then will condemn us? No one—for Christ Jesus died for us
and was raised to life for us, and he is sitting in the place of
honor at God's right hand, pleading for us.

ROMANS 8:33–34

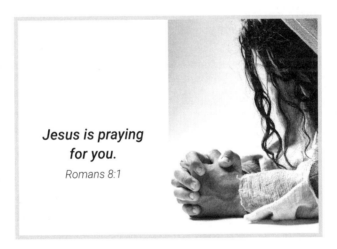

Jesus is praying
for you.
Romans 8:1

Close your eyes and form a mental picture of a courtroom. The words the apostle Paul uses in Romans 8:33–34 are legal terms; they're words you might hear inside a courtroom. In fact, we still use these words: "accuse" and "condemn."

Imagine standing in this courtroom. You feel intimidated by your surroundings. You look around and see the faces of people who have spoken against you. They've been harsh and cruel, critical, and judgmental. You see the ones who have hurt, abandoned, and neglected you. It seems as if everyone is there to accuse and condemn you.

Suddenly, Jesus enters the courtroom. You see his flowing robes, sandaled feet, and bearded face. Rather than taking his place behind the judge's bench, Jesus stands by your side. He slowly eases his arm around your shoulder and gently leads you to join him, kneeling in prayer.

You listen carefully and discover—Jesus is praying for you! He's interceding for the needs in your life, and then you hear him ask, "Where are your accusers?" You glance up and suddenly realize that the courtroom is completely empty. Everyone who was filled with condemnation has disappeared from the room. Each person who brought a charge against you has vanished. Everyone who responded with neglect or abandonment is gone. Jesus then proclaims, "Neither do I accuse you."

Let the truth of this scene impact your heart. The only One who can condemn you is praying for you! The only One who is equipped to bring judgment does not. Even as you work to reconcile hurts within your marriage, sharing confession and offering forgiveness, don't forget—the Holy One of the universe does not accuse you.

Pause and allow the Holy Spirit to fill your heart with praise and gratitude for Jesus! Your prayer might sound like Romans 8:1:

Jesus, thank you for the incomparable love that empowers you to pray for me instead of condemn me. I praise you, Jesus, because there is no condemnation for me because I am in Christ Jesus! Jesus, thank you for . . .

W6. A Spirit-empowered disciple consistently expects God to bring about life change, as the powerful presence of Jesus is encountered in the Bible.

DAY 35

Concentric Circles of Great Commission Living
(Empowered by Great Commandment Love)

Marriage Staff Meeting

This is our great commission from Jesus:

> *"Therefore, go and make disciples of all the nations,*
> *baptizing them in the name of the Father and the Son and the Holy Spirit.*
> *Teach these new disciples to obey all the commands I have given you."*
>
> MATTHEW 28:19–20

This is where we begin to fulfill that commission:

> *Jesus replied, " 'You must love the Lord your God with all your heart, all your soul, and all*
> *your mind.' This is the first and greatest commandment. A second is equally important:*
> *'Love your neighbor as yourself.' "*
>
> MATTHEW 22:37–39

Tragically, one of the greatest threats to couples living and loving like Jesus is our increasing tendency to reorder priorities differently than God intended.

God's view of life, ministry, and influence flows out of a common center—first through our intimate relationship with Jesus and then closeness with spouse and family. After all, your spouse and family *are* your closest neighbors. Ministry and mission flow out of these abundant relationships. We call this view a concentric circle model of priorities.

Work through the experiences that follow on your own and then share them with your spouse in your Marriage Staff Meeting.

As one of Christ's followers, there are important relational priorities to which only you can give careful attention. Think of these relationships as ever expanding concentric circles.

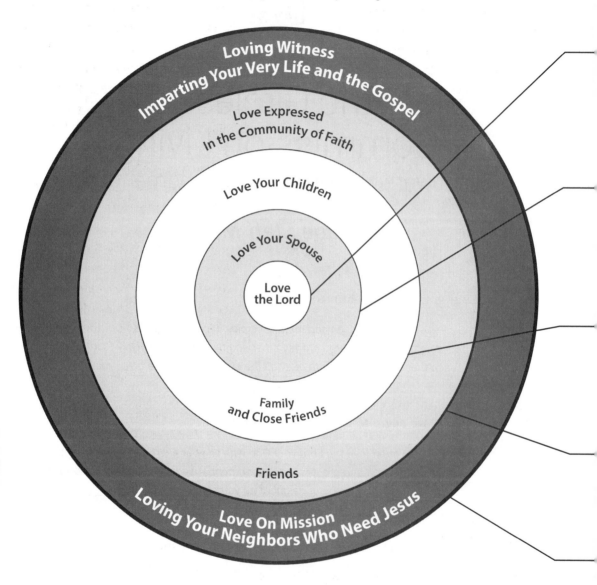

These circles are based on our Lord's Great Commission and Great Commandment. Our first priority is to love the Lord (the most center circle), love our nearest ones (circles 2–4), and finally reach the world as we live out our calling to make disciples (circle 5). This concentric circle model of priorities reflects the heart of our Lord and his intended order.

Love the Lord: The center circle (our first priority) is to live out our calling to "love the Lord with all our heart, soul, strength, and mind." We prioritize this through daily experiences in the Lord's presence with a grateful and listening heart (Matthew 22:37–38; 1 John 4:19).

Love Your Spouse: This next circle of priority literally means that you are called to "love your 'near one' as yourself." This is why 1 Peter 3:7 encourages husbands to "dwell with our wives with understanding." Wives are reminded to cherish their husbands as "a good and perfect gift" coming from the Father himself (James 1:17).

Love Your Children/Family/Friends: After your spouse, the Lord intends for your next highest calling to be the demonstration of love for your kids. Extended family members and close friends are also recipients of his love (Psalm 127:3; Proverbs 27:17).

Love in Community: The fourth circle is love expressed in the community of faith. Loving his people is an expression of the depth of love you've experienced in the first three inner circles (John 13:34–35; 2 Timothy 2:2).

Love on Mission: The outermost circle is imparting your life and the gospel. Paul modeled this in 1 Thessalonians 2:8 by saying, "We were well-pleased to impart to you not only the gospel of God but also our own lives" (NASB; also Acts 4:12).

The Concentric Circle Model of Priorities reminds us that relevant discipleship or living out our calling to love like Jesus does not begin with doctrines or teaching, behavioral standards, or performance, but with loving the Lord with all your heart, mind, soul, and strength and then loving the people closest to you.

Matthew 22:37–40 gives us the first and greatest commandment. Our call to love starts where the Great Commandment tells us to start: We must first learn to deeply love the Lord and to express his love to the "nearest ones"— our spouse, family, friends, church, and community (and in that order).

Pause and reflect on how well you are expressing your:

- Love for the Lord
- Love for your spouse
- Love for your children/ family and friends
- Love for your community
- Love for your mission as you share with those who need Jesus

My Transformation Story

Take time now to reflect on the changes you have seen in your marriage and in your personal life. In what ways has Jesus' care for you brought transformation?

- As you have received Christ's patience toward you (2 Thessalonians 3:5), have you been empowered to be patient toward your spouse?

- As you have embraced God's forgiveness for your shortcomings (Colossians 3:13), have you been empowered to forgive the shortcomings of your partner?

- As you have experienced the Lord's kindness (Romans 3:24) and accepted his gentle and humble care for you (Matthew 11:29), have you been empowered to be kind, gentle, and humble toward your spouse?

As I have received more of Christ's _____ toward me, I have been empowered to . . .

Remember:

Fresh encounters with Jesus bring about transformation.

Frequent experiences of Scripture move us beyond just *intellectually knowing* God's principles for relationships. Only when we do the Bible can God's Word make a difference.

Faithful engagement in authentic community (beginning with your spouse) brings encouragement and accountability.

These keys are the same keys for continued change in your marriage.

Reflect on your *Called 2 Love* journey and how change has come through:

- Your encounters with Jesus.

- Your experiences of specific Bible verses.

- Your engagement in authentic community with your spouse.

Write about these moments here:

I felt especially loved by Jesus when we encountered how he . . . (pursues us; uncon-
ditionally accepts us; prays for us). Jesus' love has changed me because . . .

I have changed how I _____ because we experienced specific Bible verses.
God's Word has changed me by . . .

I have changed because of the increased closeness and community with my spouse.
I've changed in these ways . . .

Living Out My Call to Love

Consider how the Lord might want you to share with others what he has done. Ask God to show you a person or a couple who could benefit from hearing this good news.

God, who might need to hear my story of how you have changed me and are trans-
forming me? Show me, Lord. I am listening.

ASK GOD TO HELP YOU INITIATE CONVERSATIONS THAT ALLOW YOU TO:

Listen to someone's story.

Say something like: *"Hey, tell me how things are going in your relationship with _____*
_____."

Share your story.

Say something like: *"There have been times in our marriage when* _____.
But Jesus is making such a difference because . . ."

Then bridge to the Jesus story.

Say something like: *"There have been times when I was too busy to go to Jesus. I was at
risk of losing_____. Jesus has helped me get my priorities straight. It's his love for me that's
enabled me to_____. Can I tell you more about Jesus?"*

 M8. A Spirit-empowered disciple actively engages in another's life story so that a personal
story of transformation can be shared; tells how Jesus has made a difference in life.

CALLED 2 LOVE MEANS:

- Asking God to make you more AWARE—acknowledge your growth areas, work on your brokenness, agree with God, rely on the Holy Spirit, and expect a transformed life.

- Continually asking God to change you and make you more like him so you are better equipped to live out his call to love.

- Being attentive, intentional, and need-focused in your relationship with your spouse—including in your sexual intimacy.

- Initiating conversations that allow you to share the hope that is in you because of Christ.

MARRIAGE INTIMACY IS DEEPENED AS YOU CONTINUE DOING THE BIBLE AND EXPERIENCING:

- Romans 14:12—always giving an account of yourself to God.

- 1 John 2:27—because the Holy Spirit lives within you, allow him to teach you and train you so you remain in fellowship with Christ.

- 1 Corinthians 7:3–5—fulfilling your spouse's sexual needs.

- 1 Thessalonians 2:8—sharing the good news of Jesus and the story of your life.

- Romans 8:1—embracing the truth that there is no condemnation in Christ Jesus.

- Matthew 22:37–39—loving the Lord and loving your nearest ones.

YOUR RELATIONSHIP WITH JESUS IS DEEPENED AS YOU:

- Imagine Christ declaring your worth and importance to him and embrace the truth that you are God's beloved.

- Imagine God wanting good things for you and your marriage relationship.

- Imagine Jesus praying for you.

WEEK FIVE

DAY 36

Marriage: The Ideal Church

This is a great mystery, but it is an illustration
of the way Christ and the church are one.

EPHESIANS 5:32

In the remaining days of our *Called 2 Love* journey, we will chronicle some of what seems to be taking place within the body of Christ—his church. There is a move of God to lead struggling couples to the kind of freedom and journey toward intimacy that the Uhlmann's and Ferguson's have enjoyed.

Prayerfully consider your role as a marriage champion and how you might expand a *Called 2 Love* model for marriage within your church and community. After all, marriage as God designed it is actually the ideal church!

You will find several important features in this final week of *Called 2 Love*.

- **Daily Devotionals**

  You will continue your daily moments of reflection and prayer with the Lord.

- **Assessments for each of the Top Ten Relational Needs**

  You will assess the significance of each relational need in your own life and then how well you're doing at meeting it for your spouse. You will also discover what it looks like and sounds like to meet each need in practical ways.

- **A structured framework for how to share your *Called 2 Love* journey with others**

  You will learn how to share your marriage story with those who are Pain-filled, Preoccupied, and Prodigals; those who need to know Jesus and the hope he brings to life and marriage.

- An Approval Exercise that is an ideal way to close out your *Called 2 Love* journey.

Making Disciples Who Make Disciples Who Make Disciples

Robert E. Webber, in his book *Ancient-Future Evangelism: Making Your Church a Faith-Forming Community*, reminds us that in 1999, some 450 church leaders from 54 countries and nearly 90 Christian fellowships and denominations gathered to address the dilemma of the church's struggle to disciple its people in Christlikeness. The gathering was called the International Consultation on Discipleship. In their report, they published these findings:

- Many converts to Christianity throughout the world fall away from faith.

- The church is marked by a paradox of growth without depth.

- Many within the church are not living lives of biblical purity, integrity, and holiness.

In addressing the participants of the International Consultation on Discipleship, noted church statesman the late John Stott said that evangelicals have "experienced enormous statistical growth . . . without corresponding growth in discipleship." African theologian Tokunboh Adeyemo lamented that the church "is one mile long, but only one inch deep."

While there appears to be a consensus among church leaders that discipleship is about growing into Christlikeness, a larger question remains: "What does Christlikeness look like in the life of a disciple of Jesus, notably a Christian married couple?"

While it might seem encouraging that the vast majority of Christian leaders, and even professed Christians, believe Christlikeness is a top priority, the problem is how professed Christians and church leaders actually define what their commitment to Christlikeness looks like.

Seventy-five percent of pastors surveyed by the Barna Group couldn't define the process toward Christlikeness except to say "obey the teachings of the Bible." The same Barna study revealed that 81 percent of professed Christians in America believe being discipled in Christ is about "trying harder to follow the rules of the Bible."*

* Barna Research Group, "Many Churchgoers and Faith Leaders Struggle to Define Spiritual Maturity," May 11, 2009, https://www.barna.com/research/many-churchgoers-and-faith-leaders-struggle-to-define-spiritual-maturity/.

Jesus never made "trying harder to follow the rules" of Scripture the main criteria of being his follower. Trying harder through obedience, discipline, and commitment doesn't characterize the biblical process of being a disciple of Christ. The "try harder" approach better describes the process held by the Pharisees of Jesus' time. The religious leaders focused on strict adherence of scriptural rules but showed little regard for others.

Jesus himself made the correct focus clear to his disciples. He said that the greatest commandment was to love God with our everything and love our neighbor as ourselves. Jesus lived a life of other-focused love and said, "Just as I have loved you, you should love each other" (John 13:34). His own definition of being like him was to live and love like him.

DISCIPLESHIP AND MARRIAGE

Loving your spouse like Jesus loves and living out his calling will include very specific, observable, and intentional steps. One way to continue our call to love is to live out our calling around the Top Ten Relational Needs. Living out an other-focused love will be evident as we live out the "one another's" of Scripture.

So let's continue the *Called 2 Love* journey by taking the following assessments and discussing them with your spouse or small group. Each assessment focuses on one of the top ten relational needs. You will:

- Assess each relational need and how important it is to you.

- Assess how well you're doing at meeting each relational need for your spouse.

- Be challenged to live out each relational need in practical and Christlike ways.

Loving your spouse as Jesus loves involves *accepting* him or her as Christ has accepted you and taking initiative to express caring *affection*.

Let's begin by assessing the need for *acceptance*. The assessment for *affection* will follow.

P3. A Spirit-empowered disciple consistently discerns the relational needs of others and shares God's love in meaningful ways.

ASSESS THE NEED FOR ACCEPTANCE

- **ACCEPTANCE**
  Assessing Our Own Need for Acceptance
  "Accept one another, then, just as Christ accepted you, in order to bring praise to God" (Romans 15:7 NIV).

  Instructions: Respond to the questions below by placing the appropriate number beside each item. Then add up your score in order to assess the significance of your relational need for acceptance.

Strongly Disagree 1	Disagree 2	Not Sure 3	Agree 4	Strongly Agree 5
_____	It is important to me that people receive me for who I am—even if I am a little different.			
_____	When I fail, it is important that others reassure me that I am still loved.			
_____	When I am introduced into a new environment, I typically search for a group with which I can connect.			
_____	It bothers me when people are prejudiced against someone just because they dress or act differently.			
_____	It is important for me to feel like I am a part of the group.			
_____	I spend a lot of time thinking about what others think of me.			
	Total			

6—12: The need for acceptance is not very significant to you.

13—21: The need for acceptance is somewhat significant to you.

22—30: The need for acceptance is very significant to you.

ASSESS THE NEED FOR ACCEPTANCE

- **ACCEPTANCE**
  Assessing How Well We Meet Others' Need for Acceptance

  Instructions: Respond to the questions below by placing the appropriate number beside each item. Then add up your score in order to assess how well you are meeting others' relational need for acceptance.

Strongly Disagree 1	Disagree 2	Not Sure 3	Agree 4	Strongly Agree 5
_____	I go out of my way to welcome those whose physical appearance, lifestyle, and/or beliefs differ from my own.			
_____	When I am in a group of people, I try to spot those who seem to be uneasy or alone and take steps to help them feel welcome.			
_____	I try to look beyond people's faults and minister to their needs.			
_____	I accept people not only when they are "up," but also when they are "down."			
_____	When others "blow it," mess up, or offend me, I am quick to forgive them.			
_____	I genuinely like all kinds of people and tend to get along well with others.			
	Total			

6—12: You need to be more thoughtful about others' need for acceptance.

13—21: You are somewhat effective at meeting others' need for acceptance.

22—30: Meeting others' need for acceptance is one of your strengths.

Acceptance: Receiving others willingly and unconditionally (even when their behavior has been imperfect) and loving them in spite of any differences that may exist between you.

We all have the need for others to accept us for who we are, "warts and all." When we accept one another, we are experiencing Romans 15:7: "Accept one another just as Christ has accepted you; then God will be glorified" (NIV). Genuine acceptance is able to separate the person from his or her behavior just as Christ loved and accepted us in spite of our sin.

What might the need for acceptance sound like?

At its core, your partner's need for acceptance may sound something like this: "Please allow me to make mistakes, and love me anyway. Allow me to be unique and not always like you. I know I'm not perfect, but I need you to look beyond my failures and imperfection and love me for who I am. I always need ten times more positive feedback than constructive criticism."

What might it sound like to give acceptance?

When your partner does something different from how you would do it, makes a mistake, or in some way fails to do what you might both agree is the "right" thing to do, acceptance will focus on the person you love, not the difference or failure:

- "Even if nothing about you changed, I would love you anyway, just the way you are."

- "I want to know how you're feeling, because how you feel is important to me."

- "For me, you are perfect."

- "What happened to the car doesn't matter to me; I'm just glad you're all right because you are what matters to me."

What might acceptance look like?

After a disagreement or a clash of wills, your acceptance might take the form of fixing your partner a favorite meal, sending a bouquet of flowers, initiating a loving conversation, or dropping the subject and not bringing it up again. Acceptance will include any gesture that communicates, "We may not see eye to eye, but I will always love you."

How might you plan to give more acceptance to your spouse?

I plan to . . .

WEEK SIX

ASSESS THE NEED FOR AFFECTION

- **AFFECTION**
  Assessing Our Own Need for Affection
  "Greet one another with a holy kiss" (Romans 16:16 NIV).
  "And he took the children in his arms, placed his hands on them and blessed them" (Mark 10:16 NIV).

  Instructions: Respond to the questions below by placing the appropriate number beside each item. Then add up your score in order to assess the significance of your relational need for affection.

Strongly Disagree 1	Disagree 2	Not Sure 3	Agree 4	Strongly Agree 5
_____	It is important to me that I receive hugs and warm embraces.			
_____	It means a lot to me when loved ones say, "I love you."			
_____	I like to be greeted with a handshake or other appropriate friendly touch.			
_____	I am a person who likes caring touch.			
_____	I am blessed when I receive unmerited, spontaneous expressions of love.			
_____	The physical aspect of marriage is/would be very important to me.			
	Total			

    6—12: The need for affection is not very significant to you.
    13—21: The need for affection is somewhat significant to you.
    22—30: The need for affection is very significant to you.

ASSESS THE NEED FOR AFFECTION

- **AFFECTION**
  Assessing How Well We Meet Others' Need for Affection

  Instructions: Respond to the questions below by placing the appropriate number beside each item. Then add up your score in order to assess how well you are meeting others' relational need for affection.

Strongly Disagree 1	Disagree 2	Not Sure 3	Agree 4	Strongly Agree 5
_____	I generously offer appropriate physical gestures of love and tenderness.			
_____	I tell people, "I love you" or "I care for you."			
_____	I welcome people by offering warm greetings and expressions of care.			
_____	I vulnerably share my heart with others and tell them that they are dear to me.			
_____	I strive to be aware of the ways in which others prefer to receive affection.			
_____	I try to consistently offer smiles and kind words, even to strangers and casual acquaintances.			
	Total			

6—12: You need to be more thoughtful about others' need for affection.

13—21: You are somewhat effective at meeting others' need for affection.

22—30: Meeting others' need for affection is one of your strengths.

Affection: Expressing care and closeness through physical touch and through words such as "I love you" or "I care about you."

We were created with the capacity and need to receive love and care through affectionate touch and loving words. When you share affection with your spouse, you are experiencing Romans 16:16: "Greet one another with a holy kiss" (NIV). Paul's words remind us that appropriate physical affection was to be an expression of loving care among believers. How much more should married couples freely share physical closeness and affectionate communication?

What might the need for affection sound like?

When your spouse has a significant need for affection, some of these words may reflect his/her perspective. "When you hold me close and speak to me tenderly, I feel loved. Your gentle touch, warm embrace, and loving words help me stay emotionally connected to you. I don't ever want your sweet words and affectionate actions to become routine."

What might it sound like to give affection?

- "You are so precious to me."
- "You mean the world to me. I don't know what I would do without you."
- "I was just thinking about how special you are to me and how much I love you."
- "I'm so happy to be with you."
- "I feel so close to you."

What might affection look like?

In a marriage relationship, embraces, private winks, loving smiles, hand-holding, kisses, and back rubs have great need-meeting value, even when they do not lead to sex—maybe particularly when they do not lead to sex. Affection may look like a quiet, romantic walk, sitting close on a park bench, listening to love songs together, or staying close while talking in a larger group.

How might you plan to give more affection to your spouse?

I plan to . . .

Engage in a *Called 2 Love* Ministry to Others

Maintaining a love-like-Jesus priority is important. It not only keeps you on your relational intimacy journey with spouse and family, it also allows you to be a shining witness to a world in need of real love. Many of your friends may be hurting and in need of someone who genuinely cares. You and your spouse can provide hope and healing to friends and family in need.

Each of us, in some way, can identify with the man Jesus encountered in the Gospel of John (John 9:1–41). We're never told the man's name, but we discover a great deal about his life. The man born blind endured significant and *painful life events*—he was born blind. There is no explanation as to why the blindness occurred; it just happened. There's often no explanation for the stuff that happens in people's lives; it just hurts.

The man also knew the hurt of *painful relationships*. He experienced the pain of rejection from neighbors and community leaders. The man's own family even seemed to lack understanding and support. The very people he expected to love, support, and protect him didn't.

In the Gospel story, we read how Jesus restored the blind man's sight, but then the man experienced the *pain of irrelevant religion*. Religious leaders didn't celebrate the miraculous healing. Instead, they put the man on trial, leaving him rejected, defensive, and alone.

REFLECT ON PEOPLE AROUND YOU:

Reflect on the friends and family who are in your life. Who may have experienced painful life events, encountered unsupportive relationships, or irrelevant religious experiences?

Identify the pain or difficulty of a friend or family member in need right now. *I'm wondering if he or she might be feeling/needing* . . .

How might you minister to his or her need and demonstrate your care for this person?

Now consider your role as a *Called 2 Love* marriage mentor. This might mean meeting weekly with another couple and sharing your marriage story. As they hear your story, invite them to experience their own 40-day journey into marriage intimacy. Invite them to go through this resource along with you.

 M1. A Spirit-empowered disciple actively does life with others and tells them about Jesus.

DAY 37

A Relational Model of Discipleship

*"I pray that they will all be one, just as you and I are one—as you are in me,
Father, and I am in you...May they experience such perfect unity that the
world will know that you sent me and that you love them as much as you love me."*

JOHN 17:21, 23

Growing in Christlikeness and building Christ-centered marriages isn't a set of rules to follow but a love relationship to enjoy. What *is* the relational model that best depicts a disciple of Christ? It's the marriage relationship as God designed it. He wants your marriage to represent him to the world!

Your earthly marriage bears the spiritual image of a loving, intimate relationship between the Father, Son, and Holy Spirit. It is this kind of loving connection that leads to a relational intimacy that others want. This kind of love is what actually draws people to Christ.

Imagine your marriage as an example of divine unity as you mutually share *appreciation* and *approval* with one another. Use the assessments from Day 36 to guide your giving to others.

Assess the needs of appreciation and approval now.

ASSESS THE NEED FOR APPRECIATION

- **APPRECIATION**
  Assessing Our Own Need for Appreciation
  "I praise you for remembering me in everything and for holding to the teachings, just as I passed them on to you" (1 Corinthians 11:2).

  Instructions: Respond to the questions below by placing the appropriate number beside each item. Then add up your score in order to assess the significance of your relational need for appreciation.

Strongly Disagree 1	Disagree 2	Not Sure 3	Agree 4	Strongly Agree 5
_____	When I have worked hard on something, I am pleased when others express gratitude.			
_____	It is encouraging to me when others notice my effort or accomplishments.			
_____	I am blessed when a superior says, "Good job."			
_____	I appreciate trophies, plaques, or special gifts as permanent reminders of something that I have done.			
_____	I enjoy receiving written notes and other specific expressions of gratitude.			
_____	I am blessed when others focus on what I have done right rather than on my mistakes.			
	Total			

6—12: The need for appreciation is not very significant to you.

13—21: The need for appreciation is somewhat significant to you.

22—30: The need for appreciation is very significant to you.

ASSESS THE NEED FOR APPRECIATION

- **APPRECIATION**

  Assessing How Well We Meet Others' Need for Appreciation

  Instructions: Respond to the questions below by placing the appropriate number beside each item. Then add up your score in order to assess how well you are meeting others' relational need for appreciation.

Strongly Disagree 1	Disagree 2	Not Sure 3	Agree 4	Strongly Agree 5
_____	I commend others for doing well or putting forth effort.			
_____	I write notes thanking others for what they do for me.			
_____	I take note of special times in people's lives when they should be commended.			
_____	I focus on what people do right rather than on what they do wrong.			
_____	I strive to be aware of the ways in which others prefer to receive appreciation (public or private, written or verbal, and so on).			
_____	I often go out of my way to thank people for their acts of service even when I have not directly benefited from their actions.			
	Total			

6—12: You need to be more thoughtful about others' need for appreciation.

13—21: You are somewhat effective at meeting others' need for appreciation.

22—30: Meeting others' need for appreciation is one of your strengths.

Appreciation: Expressing thanks, praise, or commendation, particularly in recognition of someone's accomplishments or efforts.

We all need to sense that others not only notice the things we've done or ways we've contributed, but also acknowledge and appreciate our efforts. When you express appreciation to your spouse, you are experiencing Paul's commendation in 1 Corinthians

11:2: "I praise you because you remember me in everything and hold firmly to the traditions" (NASB). Meeting the need for verbalized praise and loving appreciation in your partner will deepen the intimacy of your relationship. And as you appreciate your spouse, you are appreciating your Savior and friend, Jesus Christ.

What might the need for appreciation sound like?

Whether or not your spouse has verbalized it to you, his or her need for appreciation might sound something like this: "Please let me know when you appreciate what I do for you, even the little things that can be overlooked or taken for granted. It will mean a lot to me if you acknowledge my efforts as well as my accomplishments. Sometimes I need to sense your appreciation in tangible ways too. Your gift of gratitude is meaningful when you share it with me personally as well as when you share it in front of others."

What might it sound like to give appreciation?

Your words of appreciation might include sentences like these:

- "Kids, your mom is awesome! Look at the delicious dinner she has prepared!"
- "You cleaned the garage while I was out of town! I'm so thankful."
- "You always remember to open doors for me. I just want you to know I notice; I love it, and I don't take it for granted."
- "I'm totally impressed by how quickly you learned how to do that. You've got skills."

What might it look like to give appreciation?

Verbalized praise can be shared on small notes left in conspicuous places like a bathroom mirror, refrigerator door, car steering wheel, or cell phone. You can communicate thoughtful words of appreciation using greeting cards, letters, emails, and text messages. Nonverbal gratitude may include an enthusiastic hug, specially chosen gift, or surprise date.

How might you plan to give more appreciation to your spouse?

I plan to . . .

ASSESS THE NEED FOR APPROVAL

- **APPROVAL**

  Assessing Our Own Need for Approval

  "Do not let any unwholesome talk come out of your mouths, but only what is helpful for building others up according to their needs, that it may benefit those who listen" (Ephesians 4:29 NIV).

  Instructions: Respond to the questions below by placing the appropriate number beside each item. Then add up your score in order to assess the significance of your relational need for approval.

Strongly Disagree 1	Disagree 2	Not Sure 3	Agree 4	Strongly Agree 5
_____	It is important to me to know where I stand with those who are have authority over me.			
_____	I like to feel that I am valuable and important to others.			
_____	It is important to me that people acknowledge me not just for what I do, but also for who I am.			
_____	I feel good when someone close to me expresses satisfaction with me.			
_____	I am blessed when people commend me for a godly characteristic that I exhibit.			
_____	Feelings of rejection or the fear of rejection have been significant in my life.			
	Total			

6—12: The need for approval is not very significant to you.

13—21: The need for approval is somewhat significant to you.

22—30: The need for approval is very significant to you.

ASSESS THE NEED FOR APPROVAL

- **APPROVAL**
Assessing How Well We Meet Others' Need for Approval

Instructions: Respond to the questions below by placing the appropriate number beside each item. Then add up your score in order to assess how well you are meeting others' relational need for approval.

Strongly Disagree 1	Disagree 2	Not Sure 3	Agree 4	Strongly Agree 5
_____	I am able to view people through God's eyes, to separate who they are from what they do.			
_____	I look beyond a person's activities and performance and caringly affirm their character, heart, and spiritual maturity.			
_____	I am quick to commend people when they have done something that is good and honorable.			
_____	I am careful to affirm those for whom I have particular responsibility (such as children or employees) when they have done well, focusing specifically on the positive character qualities that contributed to their success.			
_____	I go out of my way to tell my family members and friends how blessed I feel to be in relationship with them.			
_____	I am careful with my words, seeking always to bless others rather than causing pain or feelings of rejection.			
	Total			

6—12: You need to be more thoughtful about others' need for approval.

13—21: You are somewhat effective at meeting others' need for approval.

22—30: Meeting others' need for approval is one of your strengths.

Approval: Building up or affirming another person, particularly for who they are (as opposed to what they do); affirming both the fact and the importance of our relationship with another person.

We all need to sense that others think favorably of us, and we all need affirmation from our marriage partner. A poignant example of approval is at the baptism of Jesus when the Father spoke from heaven for everyone around to hear, "You are my Son, whom I love; with you I am well pleased" (Mark 1:11 NIV). When you seek to meet your spouse's need for approval, you are experiencing Romans 14:18: "If you serve Christ with this attitude, you will please God. And other people will approve of you, too" (NLT).

Meeting the need for approval should focus more on your spouse's intrinsic worth as God's creation than on what he or she has accomplished. Showing approval places value on your spouse's character qualities and gifts—qualities such as determination, persistence, creativity, reliability, or attention to detail. Demonstrating love through approval requires that you really know your spouse. As you seek to discern his or her attributes, gifts, and qualities, you will better know how to give approval according to the need of the moment.

What might the need for approval sound like?

Your spouse may not say these specific words but have a perspective that includes these thoughts: *I need you to appreciate me for the things I do, but I also need to know you see the kind of person I am. I need to know that you love me and are proud of me. It is important to me that you see beyond my deeds to affirm my worth and character. Finally, I need to know that our relationship and our marriage are important to you.*

What might it sound like to give approval?

Your words of approval might include:

- "Your ability to create such a warm and inviting atmosphere in our home is amazing. You have an incredible gift of hospitality."

- "You are so thorough and disciplined about our finances. I'm proud of you and how you help us stay on track."

- "I admire your creativity and attention to detail. Our garden is proof!"

- "You are an amazing man. I am so proud to be married to you."

What might it look like to give approval?

Approval may look like a warm smile, an affirming hug, a card, a note or gift. The emphasis of these gifts would be on the character qualities of your spouse rather than on specific deeds or accomplishments.

How might you plan to give more approval to your spouse?

I plan to . . .

Engage in a *Called 2 Love* Ministry to the Pain-Filled

Our call to love includes learning to listen for people in pain. Who might God want you to talk to and share your story of hope with? As you come to know of other people who struggle with panic attacks, cancer, the recent pain of divorce, or a loved one's death, how might you be a voice of comfort and compassion for them?

The good news in the story of the man born blind is that when the pain became almost unbearable—the Bible says that, "When Jesus heard what had happened, he found the man" (John 9:35). Jesus pursued the man because he cared for him so much!

The Savior heard about the blind man's pain and went to find him. Jesus is still like that. He hears about the pain of your friends and may want to involve you.

Could you do the same? Could you love others like Jesus does?

Allow your heart to respond to the good news that Jesus knows, cares, and pursues those you care about . . . and then may want to send you! Consider praying something like:

Jesus, please give me the wisdom and compassion to pursue _____ and love him or her like you love. I'm feeling particularly concerned for _____ because
_____.

Prepare for a conversation with your family member, co-worker, or friend.

NOW ASK GOD TO HELP YOU INITIATE CONVERSATIONS THAT WOULD ALLOW YOU TO:

Listen to their story.

You might say something like: *"Hey, tell me how things are going with _____."*

Share your story.

You might continue the conversation with:

"There have been times in the past when I have been consumed by painful things in my life and in my marriage. I still go through painful times, but it's easier now because I can count on God's love for me. I go to him when _____."

Then bridge to the Jesus story.

"Let me tell you about this story of a man who was born blind and what a difference Jesus made in his life. Jesus knew about all of the man's struggles and made a special effort to come and find him. I've realized that Jesus loves us in this same way, and he has supported me in my struggles. That's what has enabled me to _____."

 M8. A Spirit-empowered disciple actively engages in another's life story so that a personal story of transformation can be shared; tells how Jesus has made a difference in life.

DAY 38

Is There a Disconnect?

*"Like a city on a mountain,
glowing in the night for all to see."*

MATTHEW 5:14

In some respects it seems so simple. God loves you unselfishly, and you love him and those around you with his kind of unselfish love. That is the Great Commandment in action, that in turn results in Christlikeness.

Sadly many churches are not "glowing" in their efforts to grow Christlike disciples and Christ-centered marriages. Some time ago, a large church began a process to discover their effectiveness in making disciples to be like Christ. In the 2007 Willow Creek's Reveal study, their extensive research led the leadership to the conclusion that they had been working from the wrong assumption for more than thirty years. The leaders had assumed that if people participated in the programs and activities of the church, then that would result in spiritual maturity—people being conformed to the likeness of Christ. What was the unfortunate conclusion? The leaders' assumption had been woefully misguided!

This was a wake-up call to many church leaders. It became apparent that a profession of faith in Jesus didn't automatically translate into a passion of love like Jesus. In fact, the study went on to examine the life of the professed Christian and to research how their claim to love God translated into loving others as Jesus loves.

Two hundred and thirty-five thousand professed Christians were surveyed to identify those who considered themselves truly Christ-centered.

Of these people, 78 percent said they "very strongly agree" with the statement that "I love God more than anything else." But what is surprising was that these *spiritually mature* Christians seemed to have a disconnect between loving God and loving others. The study revealed that these Christians' "love of others" was more than *two-and-a-half-times lower* than their "love of God!"*

How could this be? In a similar way, wouldn't you think that husbands and wives who say they "love God more than anything else" ought to be those who love each other intimately?

It begins to make sense why many professed Christian marriages are hardly any different than non-Christians. Their own love for God isn't being translated into a deep love for their closest neighbor, their spouse. This indicates that somewhere along the line there have been some misplaced priorities that have resulted in a clear disconnect between loving God and loving others.

Our *Called 2 Love* journey into marriage intimacy prioritizes giving to one another's relational needs like attention and comfort. Let's assess those now.

---

*   Willow Creek Association, *Focus* (Barrington, IL: Willow Creek Resources, 2009), 104, 17; Willow Creek Association, *Follow Me* (Barrington, IL: Willow Creek Resources, 2008), 108.

ASSESS THE NEED FOR ATTENTION

- **ATTENTION**
  Assessing Our Own Need for Attention
  "But that the members [of the body] may have the same care for one another" (1 Corinthians 12:25 NASB).

  Instructions: Respond to the questions below by placing the appropriate number beside each item. Then add up your score in order to assess the significance of your relational need for attention.

Strongly Disagree 1	Disagree 2	Not Sure 3	Agree 4	Strongly Agree 5
_____	I feel good when someone "enters into my world."			
_____	It is important to me to express my thoughts and feelings to those around me.			
_____	I like it when someone wants to spend time with me.			
_____	I am blessed when someone spends time doing something with me that I really enjoy even if it is not one of their favorite activities.			
_____	I am pleased when someone listens carefully to me.			
_____	Generally speaking, I do not like a lot of solitude.			
	Total			

6—12: The need for attention is not very significant to you.

13—21: The need for attention is somewhat significant to you.

22—30: The need for attention is very significant to you.

ASSESS THE NEED FOR ATTENTION

- **ATTENTION**
  Assessing How Well We Meet Others' Need for Attention

Instructions: Respond to the questions below by placing the appropriate number beside each item. Then add up your score in order to assess how well you are meeting others' relational need for attention.

Strongly Disagree 1	Disagree 2	Not Sure 3	Agree 4	Strongly Agree 5
_____	I spend time with others in order to learn about their struggles, joys, and dreams.			
_____	I try to enter into other people's physical worlds by visiting their homes, schools, and/or places of work.			
_____	I try to enter into other people's emotional worlds by discerning their emotional states, seeking understanding, and empathizing with them.			
_____	I am a good listener—I maintain good eye contact, seek to listen carefully before I respond, and offer constructive feedback when appropriate.			
_____	I spend time doing what others enjoy doing, rather than insisting that we do what I want to do.			
_____	When I am in a group of people, I give significant amounts of time and attention to a few individuals.			
	Total			

6—12: You need to be more thoughtful about others' need for attention.
13—21: You are somewhat effective at meeting others' need for attention.
22—30: Meeting others' need for attention is one of your strengths.

Attention: Conveying appropriate interest, concern, and care; taking notice of others and making an effort to enter into their respective worlds.

We were all born with a need for others to notice us, be interested in us, and care for us. Meeting your spouse's need for attention means that you consider the needs of him or her and convey appropriate care, interest, and concern. It means caring enough to enter your partner's world, learn what is important to him or her, and become involved in your partner's life. When you meet each other's need for attention, you are experiencing God's Word as expressed in 1 Corinthians 12:25: "This makes for harmony among the members, so that all the members care for each other." And when you give this caring attention to your spouse, you are giving attention to Christ.

What might the need for attention sound like?

If your spouse could verbalize this feeling, he or she might say, "I'm eager for you to consider me and enter my world—to show an interest in what I do and what I like, to care about my dreams and aspirations. But don't show me attention just because I want you to, but because you want to, because you truly care about me."

What might it sound like to give attention?

Your words of attention might include:

- "I want to know how you feel about your latest project. How did it go?"
- "Tell me about your day."
- "What are your hopes for this holiday season?"
- "What would you like to do tonight? I'd like to do what you most want to do."
- "Anything that's important to you is important to me."

What might it look like to give attention?

You demonstrate attention when you set aside your own interests for a time and focus on doing what your spouse wants to do or say. This may take the form of asking your spouse about his or her day and listening with interest. It may mean that you sit down to watch your partner's favorite TV show together or suggest that the two of you check out the garage sales on Saturday because that's what your partner likes to do. It may mean taking a class together because it's something your partner has always wanted to do. Attention may mean leisurely sipping coffee together while you ask your spouse about his or her dreams for a family vacation or career change.

How might you plan to give more attention to your spouse?

I plan to . . .

ASSESS THE NEED FOR COMFORT

- **COMFORT**
Assessing Our Own Need for Comfort
"But that the members [of the body] may have the same care for one another" (1 Corinthians 12:25 NASB).

Instructions: Respond to the questions below by placing the appropriate number beside each item. Then add up your score in order to assess the significance of your relational need for comfort.

Strongly Disagree 1	Disagree 2	Not Sure 3	Agree 4	Strongly Agree 5
_____	I feel blessed when someone recognizes and shows concern for how I am feeling.			
_____	It is important that someone expresses care for me after I have had a hard day.			
_____	Written notes and calls expressing sympathy after a serious loss or difficulty are meaningful to me.			
_____	I typically do not want to be alone when experiencing hurt and trouble.			
_____	I appreciate it when someone tries to understand me and shows me loving concern.			
_____	It is very important to me to experience God's comfort when I am in distress.			
	Total			

6—12: The need for comfort is not very significant to you.

13—21: The need for comfort is somewhat significant to you.

22—30: The need for comfort is very significant to you.

ASSESS THE NEED FOR COMFORT

- **COMFORT**
Assessing How Well We Meet Others' Need for Comfort

Instructions: Respond to the questions below by placing the appropriate number beside each item. Then add up your score in order to assess how well you are meeting others' relational need for comfort.

Strongly Disagree 1	Disagree 2	Not Sure 3	Agree 4	Strongly Agree 5
_____	I notice when others are hurting, anxious, frustrated, or emotionally "down."			
_____	I have compassion for others and seek to enter into their emotional pain.			
_____	I communicate my care and concern for others through affirming words.			
_____	I respond to hurting people with gentle touch when appropriate.			
_____	When people are hurting, I express my feelings of sadness and hurt for them instead of giving them advice or exhortation.			
_____	It really hurts me to see people who are in pain not receiving comfort from those who are closest to them.			
	Total			

6—12: You need to be more thoughtful about others' need for comfort.

13—21: You are somewhat effective at meeting others' need for comfort.

22—30: Meeting others' need for comfort is one of your strengths.

Comfort: Caringly responding to a hurting person through words, actions, emotional responses, and physical touch; hurting with and for others in the midst of their grief or pain.

Life is full of negative and hurtful experiences: disappointments, losses, relational conflict and rejection, physical and emotional pain, etc. When your spouse has suffered some kind of painful experience, his or her need of the moment is comfort. To comfort someone means to ease the grief or pain and to provide strength and hope to go on. When you comfort your spouse, you are experiencing 2 Corinthians 1:3–4: "Blessed be the God and Father of our Lord Jesus Christ, the Father of mercies and God of all comfort, who comforts us in all our affliction so that we will be able to comfort those who are in any affliction with the comfort with which we ourselves are comforted by God" (NASB).

When your spouse is hurting in some way, comfort means identifying with that hurt and compassionately communicating your sorrow and concern. Meeting the need for comfort is not about trying to fix your spouse, solve the problem or even give helpful advice. It is not about correcting behavior or sharing a motivational pep talk. These efforts may help at times, but they do not bring comfort. Romans 12:15 instructs us first to weep with those who weep to meet the need of the moment. Any other words that need to be said can come later, after you have shown your spouse comfort.

What might the need for comfort sound like?

A spouse in need of comfort is saying, "When I'm hurting, don't try to analyze the situation, fix the problem, or give me a pep talk. Just hold me, let me feel sad, and feel sad with me. Gently reassure me that you care that I am hurting and that you love me."

What might it sound like to give comfort?

Your words of comfort might include:

- "I'm sad this happened for you."
- "That must have been very difficult for you. I'm so sorry."
- "I feel a lot of compassion right now. It makes me sad to see you hurting."
- "I'm committed to be with you during all of this."
- "I'm here for you and I love you."

What might it look like to meet the need for comfort?

Comfort may appear as a tender embrace, sitting together quietly while holding hands, or even crying with one another. Comfort might include any compassionate physical expression that soothes your spouse's pain.

How might you plan to give more comfort to your spouse?

I plan to . . .

Engage in a *Called 2 Love* Ministry to the Preoccupied

Our call to love includes listening for those around us who are preoccupied with careers, hobbies, making money, and many other good things that hinder them from seeing and following Jesus.

Jairus is one Biblical character who illustrates a life of preoccupation or challenged priorities. Since he was a religious official in the ancient village of Capernaum, Jairus undoubtedly went through his daily responsibilities: opening up the synagogue, preparing for meetings, conducting gatherings of leaders, and talking with people of the community. On more than one occasion, Jairus' busyness seemed to hinder him from relating to Jesus.

Even though the small village of Capernaum was blessed by visits from Jesus, Jairus must have been preoccupied with daily routines and a busy schedule because Scripture does not mention any previous encounters between Jesus and Jairus.

On one occasion, Jesus healed a man who was lowered through the roof by his friends and caused great controversy when he declared his sins forgiven. There is no record of Jairus' interaction with Jesus (see Luke 5:17–20).

It was Capernaum where Jesus healed Peter's mother-in-law just outside the synagogue court, just over the hill from Jairus' synagogue workplace (see Mark 1:30–31).

Very near to Capernaum, Jesus regularly taught before crowds of people, performed miracles, and fed thousands of people with only meager supplies of bread and fish (see Mark 8:1–10).

Even more dramatically, on one particular Sabbath, Jesus came from the back of the synagogue and healed a man's withered hand—just before Jairus conducted his religious services! And yet again, no record of Jairus' encounters with Jesus (see Matthew 12:9–13).

Who might God want you to talk to and share a message of hope? Ask God to empower you to have conversations that include these moments:

Listen to their story.

You might have a conversation that includes: *"Tell me more about the challenges with your schedule and family priorities."*

Share your story.

Say sentences like: *"There have been times when I have been too preoccupied to notice what was going on in my husband's/wife's life or how God was working on my behalf."*

And then bridge to the Jesus story.

You might say: *"It's amazing today to see how Jesus can be doing so much around us, and yet we are too busy to notice."*

Jairus' story in the Bible is insightful. When his daughter was sick and near death, this preoccupied religious man came looking for Jesus. Jesus spoke hope-filled words for Jairus.

Jairus found hope and then healing for his daughter that day. We have that same invitation from Jesus: Come out of your preoccupation and find hope as you believe in him!

 M8. A Spirit-empowered disciple actively engages in another's life story so that a personal story of transformation can be shared; tells how Jesus has made a difference in life.

Where Are You Going?

Where there is no vision, the people are unrestrained,
but happy is he who keeps the law.

PROVERBS 29:18 NASB

It is essential in relationships that you agree about where you are going if you want to experience oneness.

In Lewis Carroll's delightful story *Alice in Wonderland,* Alice encounters the grinning Cheshire Cat. Confronted with an assortment of paths leading off in all directions, Alice inquires of the cat, "Would you tell me, please, which way I ought to go from here?"

"That depends a good deal on where you want to get to," replies the Cat.

"I don't much know or care where," Alice says.

The Cheshire Cat insightfully responds, "Then it really doesn't matter then."

Alice's exchange with the Cheshire Cat reflects the dilemma in many marriages today. "If we don't know where we're going, then any road will get us there."

Solomon said, "Where there is no vision, the people perish" (Proverbs 29:18). The Hebrew word for *perish* in this verse is also translated "go unrestrained, each to his own way."

Marriages need a clear and definite direction. So take the next few moments to assess your relationship with your spouse and agree about where you want your relationship to go.

Embrace the common vision and pathway of expressing consistent encouragement and respect.

ASSESS THE NEED FOR ENCOURAGEMENT

- **ENCOURAGEMENT**

  Assessing Our Own Need for Encouragement

  "Therefore encourage one another and build each other up"
  (1 Thessalonians 5:11 NIV).

  "And let us consider how we may spur one another on toward love and good deeds" (Hebrews 10:24 NIV).

  Instructions: Respond to the questions below by placing the appropriate number beside each item. Then add up your score in order to assess the significance of your relational need for encouragement.

Strongly Disagree 1	Disagree 2	Not Sure 3	Agree 4	Strongly Agree 5
_____	I sometimes become "weary in well doing."			
_____	I am blessed when a friend calls to listen and encourage me.			
_____	I sometimes feel overwhelmed with all I have to do.			
_____	I am blessed when someone shows interest in what I am working on.			
_____	Knowing that someone is praying for me is meaningful to me.			
_____	It is meaningful to me when others express their belief in me and urge me to pursue my goals and dreams.			
	Total			

6—12: The need for encouragement is not very significant to you.

13—21: The need for encouragement is somewhat significant to you.

22—30: The need for encouragement is very significant to you.

ASSESS THE NEED FOR ENCOURAGEMENT

- **ENCOURAGEMENT**

  Assessing How Well We Meet Others' Need for Encouragement

  Instructions: Respond to the questions below by placing the appropriate number beside each item. Then add up your score in order to assess how well you are meeting others' relational need for encouragement.

Strongly Disagree 1	Disagree 2	Not Sure 3	Agree 4	Strongly Agree 5
_____	I try to anticipate times and situations in which people may be discouraged so that I can encourage them.			
_____	I go out of my way to call, write, or visit those who are discouraged, disappointed, or struggling.			
_____	I encourage others to develop a positive vision and realistic goals and then support them in their journey.			
_____	I faithfully pray for people, both privately and with them.			
_____	I encourage others by expressing sincere confidence in God's work in and through them.			
_____	I feel great compassion for those who are overwhelmed by the demands of their lives.			
	Total			

6—12: You need to be more thoughtful about others' need for encouragement.

13—21: You are somewhat effective at meeting others' need for encouragement.

22—30: Meeting others' need for encouragement is one of your strengths.

Encouragement: Urging others to persist and persevere in their efforts to attain their goals; stimulating others toward love and good deeds.

Everybody gets discouraged at times, particularly when we lose sight of a goal or lose hope through disappointment, frustration, rejection or failure. In your spouse's moments of discouragement, the need of the moment is for encouragement. As you encourage your partner, you supply the needed motivation to go on and inspire courage, spirit and hope. And you are experiencing Hebrews 10:24–25: "Let us consider how we may spur one another on toward love and good deeds, . . . encouraging one another" (NIV).

What might the need for encouragement sound like?

When your partner needs encouragement, here's what his or her heart is saying: "When I feel discouraged or disappointed, I need you to assure me that everything is all right and help me get back on track. I need you to lift my spirits and share your confidence that I can still reach my goals. You encourage me by helping me see the light at the end of the tunnel."

What might it sound like to give encouragement?

Your words of encouragement might include:

- "I know this is a difficult time for you, but I believe in you."
- "What can I do to help you accomplish your goals this week?"
- "So many people are going to be positively impacted by your good work on this project. I know you will finish it because you believe in it."
- "If anyone can do this, it's you!"
- "Tomorrow is a new day, and I am excited to experience it with you."

What might it look like to give encouragement?

When your spouse is feeling down, you may share your encouragement in the form of a reassuring smile, a cold glass of lemonade, or an uplifting note. Being available to spend time praying with your spouse, discussing his or her options, or just sitting together and talking through the challenges may provide encouragement. Or it might help to offer a fun diversion, such as dinner out, a drive in the country, a get-together with friends, or time of prayer.

How might you plan to give more encouragement to your spouse?

I plan to . . .

ASSESS THE NEED FOR RESPECT

- **RESPECT**
  Assessing Our Own Need for Respect
  "Honor one another above yourselves" (Romans 12:10 NIV).
  "Show proper respect to everyone" (1 Peter 2:17 NIV).

  Instructions: Respond to the questions below by placing the appropriate number beside each item. Then add up your score in order to assess the significance of your relational need for respect.

Strongly Disagree 1	Disagree 2	Not Sure 3	Agree 4	Strongly Agree 5
_____	It is vital to me that others ask me my opinion.			
_____	I resist being seen only as a part of a large group—my individuality is important to me.			
_____	I want to be treated with kindness and equality by all regardless of my race, gender, looks, or status.			
_____	When a decision is going to affect me, it is important that I be involved in the decision making process.			
_____	I am bothered by people who are controlling.			
_____	It is very important to me that people have appropriate respect for my things and my space.			
	Total			

6—12: The need for respect is not very significant to you.

13—21: The need for respect is somewhat significant to you.

22—30: The need for respect is very significant to you.

ASSESS THE NEED FOR RESPECT

- **RESPECT**

  Assessing How Well We Meet Others' Need for Respect

  Instructions: Respond to the questions below by placing the appropriate number beside each item. Then add up your score in order to assess how well you are meeting others' relational need for respect.

Strongly Disagree 1	Disagree 2	Not Sure 3	Agree 4	Strongly Agree 5
_____	Before making a decision, I solicit input from those whose lives will be impacted by the decision.			
_____	I have regard for others people's ideas, opinions, and perspectives, even when they differ from my own.			
_____	I respect other people's personal property and privacy.			
_____	I treat everyone with dignity and courtesy regardless of their race, lifestyle, or socio-economic status.			
_____	I am careful to be on time to appointments and meetings.			
_____	In group settings, it is important to me that each individual is given a chance to express his or her thoughts and opinions.			
	Total			

6—12: You need to be more thoughtful about others' need for respect.

13—21: You are somewhat effective at meeting others' need for respect.

22—30: Meeting others' need for respect is one of your strengths.

Respect: Valuing one another highly, treating one another as important, and honoring one another with our words and actions.

We all need people to value us, to recognize our worth, and to esteem us. You communicate esteem when you respect your spouse's ideas, opinions, wishes, personal space, and schedule and when you seek your partner's perspective on an issue or decision. You convey worth when you affirm his or her strengths and abilities. When you respect your spouse, you are experiencing 1 Peter 2:17: "Respect everyone, and love the family of believers. Fear God, and respect the king." And respect shown to your spouse is respect shown to Christ.

What might the need for respect sound like?

Your partner has a need for respect. Here are some things he or she might want to say: "It means so much to me when you ask for my advice or opinion, when you involve me when making plans for us, and when you talk to me before making plans that affect me or my schedule. The tone of voice you use with me is very important. I feel disrespected if anyone talks down to me, is harsh or sarcastic. Treating me with value and honor is critical for me."

What might it sound like to give respect?

Your words of respect might include:

- "You're so good at helping me think through details. I need your input."

- "May I share what I'm dealing with so you can tell me what you think?"

- "What do you think we should do? I'd really like to get your opinion."

- "We may have to change plans, but I wanted to talk it through with you first."

What might it look like to give respect?

Respect may be demonstrated through being punctual and respecting your partner's schedule. It may mean allowing your spouse time alone, respecting his need for personal space, or staying within the family budget. Respect may also include caring for your spouse's personal property, valuing her ideas, or asking his opinion.

How might you plan to give more respect to your spouse?

I plan to . . .

Engage in a *Called 2 Love* Ministry to the Prodigals

"But while he was still a long way off,
his father saw him and was filled with compassion for him;
he ran to his son, threw his arms around him and kissed him."

LUKE 15:20

This section is about reflecting on the prodigal story and how it can cultivate compassion for other people—people beyond your marriage.

Jesus' story of the prodigal returning home is of great relevance in our world today. Self-focus is the first thing we see: "Give me, give me what is mine."

Next, the prodigal visits places he should not have been and squanders precious things.

We've all been self-focused at time, visited places and entertained relationships that were not helpful. So have many of our friends. We have all squandered precious opportunities, time, and relationships. So have our family members.

Having grown empty and lonely, the prodigal decides to go home. Picture him walking along dusty, winding roads. Finally, he turns the last corner and catches a glimpse of a familiar home in the distance.

In order to minister to prodigals outside of your marriage relationship, picture Jesus waiting for you and your friend to return home. When he sees you both in the distance, he is moved with compassion, and he runs toward you. Picture Jesus leaping off the front porch because he cannot wait to see you and your fellow prodigal. He embraces and speaks blessings to you. Jesus does not offer lectures or criticism. There is no rebuke or scorn. His voice is filled with compassion, forgiveness, acceptance, and care.

This is what it means to love like Jesus. This is what it looks like to love a prodigal. Who do you know (outside of your marriage) that needs this kind of acceptance and compassion? Who might God want you to talk to, share with, and extend this kind of love?

Ask God to prepare you for conversations with others who don't know Jesus and are living their life as a prodigal.

ASK THE HOLY SPIRIT TO EMPOWER YOU AS YOU:

Listen to their story.

You might begin a conversation in a simple way: *"Tell me more about your _____."*

Share your story.

Talk about your own experiences, such as:

- "It's sad, but I can look back on the many times I have been **selfish** and focused only on my agenda. I really hurt my family.

- I **wasted a lot of precious opportunities** to connect with my spouse and my kids because I . . .

- I lived several years **rebelling** against rules and authorities, getting into trouble, and I paid some painful consequences. My crazy story reminds me of Jesus' story about a prodigal like me."

And then bridge to the Jesus story.

"When Jesus sees you and me a long way off, he is filled with compassion. He runs toward us because he can't wait to love us."

 M8. A Spirit-empowered disciple actively engages in another's life story so that a personal story of transformation can be shared; tells how Jesus has made a difference in life.

DAY 40

Called 2 Love Like Jesus

Marriage Staff Meeting

"So now I am giving you a new commandment:
Love each other. Just as I have loved you, you should love each other."

JOHN 13:34

We hope you have grown in your understanding and amazement that God desires to permeate your marriage and revel in the joy of the relationship between you and your spouse. As your marriage expresses the intimacy of love, it reveals the Father's love for his Son and his church. As your marriage portrays the oneness of caring involvement, it bears the image of the caring involvement between Father, Son, and Holy Spirit. As your marriage demonstrates the security and vulnerability of two people truly knowing and being known by one another, you give evidence and hope of God's goodness in a lonely world.

These possibilities bring great motivation for life. When we demonstrate oneness in marriage and live out our call to love, the Creator gets the praise. "Worthy is the Lamb . . . to receive power and riches and wisdom and strength and honor and glory and blessing" (Revelation 5:12). It is for his pleasure that you and your spouse were created and blessed with marriage intimacy.

Complete these final exercises privately and then share your responses with your spouse. Let this final Marriage Staff Meeting be a celebration of what God has done in and through your relationship.

"A new command I give to you, that you love one another: just as I have loved you, you also are to love one another."

JOHN 13:34 ESV

The FIRST of Three Big Life Questions

WHO IS HE?

Think about the words of John 13:34. They're a command. Now consider this: Who is the one Person who gets to issue commands? Is it the Old Testament prophets? No. How about the New Testament Pharisees? No. They could declare edicts and laws but never commands. To do so would have been to claim to be Jehovah. Jesus—the One who is God—gave us this new command. The same God who gave the first Ten Commandments to Moses gave us this commandment: To love one another just as he has loved us.

Reflect for a moment about this calling. Just as God has commanded us not to steal, murder, or covet (because he wants the best for our lives), he also commands us to love. In other words, the One in authority has given us an order. The One in authority has called us to love.

You may be asking yourself: *How am I going to be able to live out this command?*

The key to living out God's command can be found in John 13:34: "Just as I have loved you." The key to living out God's command to love others is to experience more and more of his love for us.

Doing the Bible

Because Your lovingkindness is better than life, my lips will praise You.

PSALM 63:3 NASB

Write about one of the times when you sensed God's love for you.

One of the times when I sensed God's love for me was when . . .

And my heart is moved to respond with . . .

The SECOND of Three Big Life Questions

"A new commandment I give to you, that you love one another:
just as I have loved you, you also are to love one another."

JOHN 13:34 ESV

WHO ARE YOU?

You might not yet fully believe it or feel it, but with these few words, "Just as I have loved you," Jesus declared that YOU are the BELOVED of GOD!

Reflect once more on the privilege of being born again.

Why did Christ sacrifice himself on the cross?

Even more personally, for whom did he do this?

Who benefits from Jesus' death and resurrection?

If Christ did not need to die for any other person in the whole world, he would have died for you, and he did!

Quietly listen to the Spirit whisper these words to you: *"He did it for you. He did it for you!"*
Is your heart moved with gratitude, humility, or joy?

Allow yourself a moment to respond to this glorious truth. Jesus sacrificed himself in death and then was raised for you. Allow yourself to whisper these words: *He did it for me.* Write a prayer to Jesus here.

Jesus, I am so grateful that . . .

But God demonstrates His own love toward us,
in that while we were yet sinners, Christ died for us.

ROMANS 5:8 NASB

 L4. A Spirit-empowered disciple lives joyfully and confidently in his identity as one who is loved by God and belongs to him.

The THIRD of Three Big Life Questions

"A new commandment I give to you, that you love one another:
just as I have loved you, you also are to love one another."

JOHN 13:34 ESV

WHY ARE YOU HERE?

This same passage of Scripture not only tells us who Jesus is and who we are, it also brings clarity to our life purpose. With these few words, Christ declares that life's highest calling, most important goal, and foundational purpose is to *love*.

With the words, "Love one another," Jesus declares a purpose for his people. We are called to love.

Take a moment now to recall a way in which your spouse might need to be loved. Today, make a phone call, send a text or have a quiet conversation and do what Jesus did. Take initiative, pursue your spouse, and live out your call to love.

As I think about the circumstances that my spouse is going through, one of the most meaningful ways I can love him/her like Jesus is to . . .

 P5. A Spirit-empowered disciple consistently shows family and close friends the kind of love that Jesus has for those he loves.

His Story

A transformed life is possible as we consistently connect with Jesus. We can live out our call to love as we embrace his empowering love toward us and learn from him.

As a final experience with your partner, imagine Jesus inviting you to come and join him in the yoke—learning to better love your spouse.

Imagine Jesus standing before you, gazing intently at you. Imagine the robes and sandals he might wear. Imagine his bearded face and how his eyes are full of compassion. As you look closely, you notice that Jesus is standing in a yoke. One side of the yoke is around his neck while the other is empty. Christ extends his invitation for you to join him.

WEEK SIX

If you listen closely, you hear him say, "Come and take my yoke. Let's wear it together. I am a humble and gentle teacher. I'll teach you what I know about your partner. I'll gently help you learn to love your spouse in more and more meaningful ways."

End your time with a prayer to the One who is love. Let your spouse (or small group) overhear your prayer.

Jesus, I want to join you in loving my partner well. I want you, the One who is love, to teach me and lead me. Thank you for your Spirit empowering me to love like you.

"Come to Me, all who are weary and heavy-laden, and I will give you rest.
Take My yoke upon you and learn from Me, for I am gentle and humble in heart,
and you will find rest for your souls."

MATTHEW 11:28–29 NASB

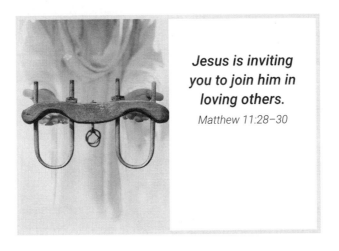

Jesus is inviting you to join him in loving others.
Matthew 11:28–30

P5. A Spirit-empowered disciple consistently shows family and close friends the kind of love that Jesus has for those he loves.

As a final step in your *Called 2 Love* journey, assess the needs for security and support and make intentional plans to meet those needs for your spouse.

ASSESS THE NEED FOR SECURITY

- **SECURITY (PEACE)**
  Assessing Our Own Need for Security
  "Live in harmony with one another . . . If it is possible, as far as it depends on you, live at peace with everyone" (Romans 12:16, 18 NIV).

  Instructions: Respond to the questions below by placing the appropriate number beside each item. Then add up your score in order to assess the significance of your relational need for security.

Strongly Disagree 1	Disagree 2	Not Sure 3	Agree 4	Strongly Agree 5
_____	It is important to me that my finances be in order.			
_____	I feel best when my world is orderly and somewhat predictable.			
_____	I sometimes worry about the future.			
_____	The thought of change produces anxiety for me.			
_____	I want my friends and loved ones to be there for me through thick and thin.			
_____	I appreciate it when those who are closest to me make decisions based on a desire to promote my well-being.			
	Total			

6—12: The need for security is not very significant to you.

13—21: The need for security is somewhat significant to you.

22—30: The need for security is very significant to you.

ASSESS THE NEED FOR SECURITY

- **SECURITY (PEACE)**
  Assessing How Well We Meet Others' Need for Security

  Instructions: Respond to the questions below by placing the appropriate number beside each item. Then add up your score in order to assess how well you are meeting others' relational need for security.

Strongly Disagree 1	Disagree 2	Not Sure 3	Agree 4	Strongly Agree 5
_____	I am open and transparent in sharing my care and concern with those to whom I am closest.			
_____	I pro-actively attempt to maintain health in all my relationships. If a relationship is strained, I try to repair it quickly.			
_____	I am even-tempered and not prone to moodiness or outbursts of anger; there is consistency in how I relate to people.			
_____	I make decisions based on the well-being of those I love and care for, not just my own well-being.			
_____	I avoid impulsive actions and decisions that might adversely affect those who depend on me.			
_____	I strive to reassure others about their future, particularly when they are facing major changes or challenges.			
	Total			

6—12: You need to be more thoughtful about others' need for security.

13—21: You are somewhat effective at meeting others' need for security.

22—30: Meeting others' need for security is one of your strengths.

Security: Establishing and maintaining harmony in our relationships and providing freedom from fear or threat of harm through expressions of vulnerability, deepening of trust, and the successful resolution of conflict.

Security defines our need for protection from danger, deprivation, and harmful relationships. We all need to experience freedom from fears and to feel safe from physical, emotional, relational, and financial peril. We need to sense that we will be provided for and cared for. We all need to sense that we can count on our spouse and trust them to make decisions that are in the best interest of our marriage and family. When we provide security for our partner, we are experiencing Psalm 122:6–8: "May those who love you be secure. May there be peace within your walls and security within your citadels. . . . I will say, 'Peace be within you'" (NIV).

What might the need for security sound like?

A spouse who needs security is saying, "I want to feel assured that everything between us is all right, that you are committed for the long haul as we grow through our differences. I want to feel safe in our financial dealings, investments, and retirement planning. I want to feel safe from harmful social relationships and physical danger."

What might it sound like to give security?

Your words of security might include:

- "I love you now, and I will always love you, no matter what happens."
- "If I could do it all over again, you are the one I would choose to spend my life with."
- "I am committed to you, and as God allows and provides, I will meet your needs both now and in the future."

What might it look like to give security?

Physical security might appear as joint ownership of all property and possessions, an updated will, promptly paying bills, a savings plan, and health, life, and disability insurance. It might also include a home security system, careful driving, or an adequate retirement plan. Relational and emotional security may include keeping promises, being dependable, setting goals for the future, and then working together to make them happen.

How might you plan to give more security to your spouse?

I plan to . . .

ASSESS THE NEED FOR SUPPORT

- **SUPPORT**
Assessing Our Own Need for Support
"Carry each other's burdens, and in this way you will fulfill the law of Christ" (Galatians 6:2 NIV).

Instructions: Respond to the questions below by placing the appropriate number beside each item. Then add up your score in order to assess the significance of your relational need for support.

Strongly Disagree 1	Disagree 2	Not Sure 3	Agree 4	Strongly Agree 5
_____	I am blessed when someone notices that I need help and offers to get involved.			
_____	When I feel overwhelmed, I want someone to come alongside me and bear my burden.			
_____	When facing something difficult, I appreciate having other people's input and assistance.			
_____	I do not enjoy undertaking a project by myself; I prefer to have a partner.			
_____	I would rather work with a team of people than by myself.			
_____	I appreciate it when others offer their time and financial resources to me in my times of need.			
	Total			

6—12: The need for support is not very significant to you.

13—21: The need for support is somewhat significant to you.

22—30: The need for support is very significant to you.

WEEK SIX

ASSESS THE NEED FOR SUPPORT

- **SUPPORT**

  Assessing How Well We Meet Others' Need for Support

  Instructions: Respond to the questions below by placing the appropriate number beside each item. Then add up your score in order to assess how well you are meeting others' relational need for support.

Strongly Disagree 1	Disagree 2	Not Sure 3	Agree 4	Strongly Agree 5
_____	I help others in their times of greatest need.			
_____	Before I give support, I ask others how I can help bear their burden.			
_____	I attend weddings, funerals, concerts, sports activities, and family events as a means of demonstrating my love for others.			
_____	I use my personal resources to help others.			
_____	I willingly defer my plans and schedule in order to be available for others.			
_____	If I see someone working alone on a project or task, I offer to lend a hand.			
	Total			

  6—12: You need to be more thoughtful about others' need for support.

  13—21: You are somewhat effective at meeting others' need for support.

  22—30: Meeting others' need for support is one of your strengths.

Support: Coming alongside others and providing gentle, appropriate assistance with a problem or struggle.

Giving support is not something you can do from a distance. Support means coming alongside your spouse and lending your shoulder to share the weight of a burden or struggle. The burden could be physical or material, such as moving furniture, addressing Christmas cards, planting a garden, or cleaning the house. Burdens can also be more relational or emotional, such as disciplining a child, making a financial decision, or dealing with a difficult friend, family member, or neighbor. When you lend your support to your partner, you are experiencing Galatians 6:2: "Carry each other's burdens, and in this way you will fulfill the law of Christ" (NIV).

What might the need for support sound like?

When your partner is struggling under a heavy load, he or she may want to communicate: "I need to know that you are available to help me in this situation and that you really want to help me. The last thing I need when I'm overburdened or stressed is to feel alone."

What might it sound like to give support?

Words like these help convey your readiness to provide support:

- "I sense you can use some help. How can support you?"
- "Is there anything I can do to help you today?"
- "If you show me what needs to be done, I'll be glad to help out."
- "I know this is tough. Let's talk it through, and would you like to pray together?"

What might it look like to give support?

You may demonstrate support by helping your spouse complete a chore, finish a project, prepare for or clean up after an event, build or repair something. To meet the need for support, you might take on extra household duties or take on more of the responsibilities with the children. You might also offer to listen compassionately while your spouse talks through a problem, concern, or fear and then assist in the solution or response.

How might you plan to give more support to your spouse?

I plan to . . .

As you conclude the *Called 2 Love* journey, you may want to consider ending your six week journey by meeting one another's need for approval. This can be a perfect exercise to conclude your final Marriage Staff Meeting, small group, or class experience.

Approval Exercise

Consider your relationship with your spouse or members of your small group, then reflect on specific aspects of approval you have for each. Begin selecting a character quality that you most admire about your spouse (and members of your small group). Choose from the list of qualities on the following pages or choose your own. Take turns sharing words of approval. If using this exercise in a small group, there is no pressure for everyone to share approval with each person, but it is important that each member has opportunity to both *receive* approval and *give* approval.

Choose the character quality and then tell about a time you've seen that quality displayed. Short sentences are normally the best.

- *"I'm grateful for your _____, especially when you _____ ." For example, "I'm grateful for your creative contribution to our family, especially when you help us have fun times together."*

- *"I love how you are so _____, for instance _____ ." For example, "I love how you are so dependable, for instance I can always count on you to keep promises and do what you say you are going to do."*

The importance of sharing approval

- Sharing approval helps keep us focused on what people are doing right.

- Hearing and receiving approval helps prompt gratitude and a good attitude.

- A home environment of approval makes life more fun and fulfilling.

- Hearing and receiving approval helps prepare us for when inevitable challenges come.

- Other people (friends, neighbors, and family members) find an approving environment appealing and attractive.

30 Selected Character Qualities

1. ACCEPTANCE—deliberate and ready reception with a favorable response; receiving someone unconditionally and willingly.

2. CAUTIOUSNESS—gaining adequate counsel before making decisions; recognizing bad choices and avoiding them.

3. COMPASSION—feeling the hurts of others and doing all that is possible to relieve them.

4. CONTENTMENT—enjoying present possessions rather than desiring new or additional ones; being happy regardless of circumstances.

5. CREATIVITY—finding "out of the box" solutions to difficult problems; discovering practical applications from life's wisdom.

6. DECISIVENESS—finalizing difficult decisions on the basis of life principles, personal values, and sound wisdom.

7. DEFERENCE—limiting our freedom to not offend but rather serve those around us.

8. DEPENDABILITY—being true to our word even when it is difficult to carry out what we promised to do.

9. DILIGENCE—seeing every task as a significant personal assignment, and applying energy and concentration to accomplish it.

10. DISCERNMENT (Sensitivity)—knowing what to look for in evaluating people, problems, and things; saying the right words at the right time.

11. ENDURANCE (Perseverance)—maintaining commitments during times of pressure.

12. FAITH—developing an unshakable confidence in what could be and acting upon it.

13. FORGIVENESS—choosing to not hold an offense against another; remembering how much we have been forgiven.

14. GENEROSITY—learning how to be a wise steward of time, money, and possessions; being cheerful in sharing what we have and who we are.

15. GENTLENESS—responding to needs with kindness and love; knowing what is appropriate to meet the emotional needs of others.

16. GRATEFULNESS—recognizing the benefits that have been provided; looking for appropriate ways to express genuine appreciation.

17. HOSPITALITY—sharing what we have with those whom we don't know; caring well for strangers.

18. HUMILITY—recognizing our inability to accomplish very much *all by ourselves*; recognizing our fundamental *neediness*.

19. INITIATIVE—acting first rather than waiting for others to give; taking appropriate action even when not asked.

20. LOYALTY—adopting as our own the wishes and goals of those we are serving.

21. MEEKNESS—yielding our rights in order to serve; being willing to earn the right to be heard rather than demanding a hearing.

22. PATIENCE —accepting difficult situations without irritation but with kindness and grace.

23. PUNCTUALITY—showing esteem for other people and their time by not keeping them waiting.

24. REVERENCE—communicating a sense of respect and *wonder* in our faith journey.

25. SECURITY—remaining trustworthy; able to be counted upon.

26. SELF-CONTROL—resisting self indulgence, self defensiveness, and fearful control; bringing our thoughts, words, and actions under control.

27. SINCERITY—having motives that are transparent; having a genuine concern to benefit the lives of others.

28. TRUTHFULNESS—risking the consequences of openness; facing the consequences of a mistake; telling the whole truth.

29. VIRTUE—demonstrating personal moral standards that challenge others to consider theirs.

30. WISDOM—seeing life from a perspective greater than our own; learning how to apply life principles in practical situations.

GOAL SETTING IS AN EXAMPLE AND WITNESS TO OTHERS

Our generation lives in a leadership vacuum with everyone looking for individuals or families who know where they're headed. Christian families can be a witness and an example by establishing goal-directed homes with a vision.

Reflect on your example to others as you answer the following questions:

How have you seen God use an area of family strength in your home to encourage or challenge others?

In what area of your life would you like to see your family become a better example?

We often find it helpful for couples to consider questions like these:

(Check (✓) the ones for which you personally have an answer.)

	What's the next special date I have planned with my spouse?
	What particular character qualities are we now emphasizing as we raise our children?
	What's the next major household expenditure we've agreed on making?
	What are our financial plans for eliminating credit card debt? For saving toward our children's college education?
	Which married couple friends are we purposefully developing close relationships with?
	What ministry dreams and plans do we share together as a couple?
	What spiritual goals are we sharing through our prayer times, devotionals, or Bible study?
	What plans do I have for personal development through education, self study, or career enhancement?

For how many of the these items do you and your partner have answers? Each one addresses your family's future and your sense of vision. The special emphasis on goal setting is designed to be explored during a get-away goal setting retreat for husbands and wives.

CALLED 2 LOVE MEANS:

- Taking initiative to give to your spouse according to his or her relational needs; becoming equipped to meet all ten relational needs for others.

- Sharing your marriage story with those who are pain-filled, preoccupied, and prodigals; sharing with those who need to know Jesus and the hope he brings to life and marriage.

- Continuing to practice the disciplines of great relationships: couple devotions, Marriage Staff Meetings, and goal setting

- Learning to meet the relational need for approval.

MARRIAGE INTMACY IS DEEPENED AS YOU CONTINUE DOING THE BIBLE AND EXPERIENCING:

- First Thessalonians 2:8—sharing the good news of Jesus and the story of your life.

- Proverbs 28:18—intentionally connecting with your spouse through Marriage Staff Meetings.

- John 13:34 —Loving your spouse in practical ways, according to the ten relational needs which are actually the "one another's" of Scripture.

YOUR RELATIONSHIP WITH JESUS IS DEEPENED AS YOU:

- Imagine Jesus inviting you to join him in loving your partner well; giving you instruction, insight, and wisdom and equipping you for loving like he loves.

- Imagine Jesus empowering you to tell your Called 2 Love story and then share the hope he brings to life and marriage.

APPENDIX 1

Relational Needs Assessment Tool

This exercise will enable you to better identify the priority of your relational needs.

Instructions:

Take time to individually respond to the following statements by placing the appropriate number beside each sentence. When you have completed all fifty statements, you may interpret your answers by using the *Identifying Your Top Needs Scoring* .

Strongly Disagree	Disagree	Neutral	Agree	Strongly Agree
1	2	3	4	5

Name: _____ Date: _____

___1.   It is important that people receive me for who I am—even if I'm a little "different."

___2.   It is important to me that my world is in order.

___3.   I sometimes grow tired of trying to do my best.

___4.   It is significant to me when others ask my opinion.

___5.   It is important that I receive frequent physical hugs, warm embraces, etc.

___6.   I feel good when someone takes a special interest in the things that are important to me.

___7.   It is important for me to know "where I stand" with those who are in authority over me.

___8.   It is meaningful when someone notices that I need help and then offers to get involved.

___9.   When I feel overwhelmed, I especially need someone to come alongside me and help.

___10. I feel pleased when someone recognizes and shows concern for how I'm feeling emotionally.

___11. I like to know that I am significant and valued by others.

___12. Generally speaking, I don't like a lot of solitude.

___13. I like it when my loved ones say to me, "I love you."

___14. I don't like being seen only as a part of a large group—my individuality is important.

___15. I am pleased when a friend calls to listen to me and encourage me.

___16. It is important to me that people acknowledge me, not just for what I do, but also for who I am.

___17. I feel best when my world is orderly and somewhat predictable.

___18. When I've worked hard on a project, I am pleased to have people acknowledge my work and express gratitude.

___19. When I "blow it," it is important to me to be reassured that I am still loved.

___20. It is encouraging to me when I realize that others notice my skills and strengths.

___21. I sometimes feel overwhelmed and discouraged.

_____ 22. It's important to me to be treated with kindness and equality, regardless of my race, gender, looks, and status.

_____ 23. To have someone I care about touch me on the arm or shoulder or give me a hug feels good.

_____ 24. I enjoy it when someone wants to spend time with just me.

_____ 25. It is meaningful when someone I look up to says, "Good job."

_____ 26. It is important to me for someone to show concern for me after I've had a hard day.

_____ 27. While I may feel confident about what I do (my talents, gifts, etc.), I also believe that I need other people's input and help.

_____ 28. Written notes and calls expressing sympathy after the death of a loved one, health problems, or other stressful events are (or would be) very meaningful to me.

_____ 29. I feel good when someone shows satisfaction with the way I am.

_____ 30. I enjoy being spoken well of or affirmed in front of a group of people.

_____ 31. I would be described as an "affectionate" person.

_____ 32. When a decision is going to affect my life, it is important to me that my input is sought and given serious consideration.

_____ 33. I am pleased when someone shows interest in current projects on which I am working.

_____ 34. I appreciate trophies, plaques, and special gifts, which are permanent reminders of something significant that I have done.

_____ 35. It is not unusual for me to worry about the future.

_____ 36. When I am introduced into a new environment, I typically search for a group of people with whom I can connect.

_____ 37. The possibility of major change (moving, new job … etc.) produces anxiety for me.

_____ 38. It bothers me when people are prejudiced against others just because they dress or act differently.

_____ 39. It is necessary for me to be surrounded by friends and loved ones who will be there through thick and thin.

_____ 40. Receiving written notes and expressions of gratitude particularly pleases me.

_____ 41. To know that someone is thinking of me is very meaningful.

_____ 42. People who try to control me or others annoy me.

_____ 43. I am pleased by unexpected and spontaneous expressions of care.

_____ 44. I feel important when someone looks me in the eye and listens to me without distractions.

_____ 45. I am grateful when people commend me for a positive characteristic I exhibit.

_____ 46. I don't like to be alone when experiencing hurt and trouble; it is important for me to have a companion who will be with me.

_____ 47. I don't enjoy working on a project by myself; I prefer to have a partner on important projects.

_____ 48. It is important for me to know I am part of the group.

_____ 49. I respond to someone who tries to understand me emotionally and who shows me caring concern.

_____ 50. When working on a project, I would rather work with a team of people than by myself.

great
commandment
network

Identifying Your Top Needs Scoring

Add up your responses corresponding to each question to find the totals related to each need.

Acceptance

1 _____
19 _____
36 _____
38 _____
48 _____
Total _____

Respect

4 _____
14 _____
22 _____
32 _____
42 _____
Total _____

Comfort

10 _____
26 _____
28 _____
46 _____
49 _____
Total _____

Security

2 _____
17 _____
35 _____
37 _____
39 _____
Total _____

Affection

5 _____
13 _____
23 _____
31 _____
43 _____
Total _____

Support

8 _____
9 _____
27 _____
47 _____
50 _____
Total _____

Appreciation

11 _____
18 _____
25 _____
34 _____
40 _____
Total _____

Attention

6 _____
12 _____
24 _____
30 _____
44 _____
Total _____

Encouragement

3 _____
15 _____
21 _____
33 _____
41 _____
Total _____

Approval

7 _____
16 _____
20 _____
29 _____
45 _____
Total _____

1. What were your three highest totals? Which needs do they represent?

2. What were your three lowest totals? Which needs do they represent?

Source: © 2011 Center for Relational Leadership, 2511 South Lakeline Blvd., Cedar Park, TX 78613

APPENDIX 2

ABOUT THE GREAT COMMANDMENT NETWORK

The Great Commandment Network is an international collaborative network of strategic kingdom leaders from the faith community, marketplace, education, and caregiving fields who prioritize the powerful simplicity of the words of Jesus to love God, love others, and see others become his followers (Matthew 22:37–40, Matthew 28:19–20).

The Great Commandment Network is served through the following:

Relationship Press – This team collaborates, supports, and joins together with churches, denominational partners, and professional associates to develop, print, and produce resources that facilitate ongoing Great Commandment ministry.

The Center for Relational Leadership – Their mission is to teach, train, and mentor both ministry and corporate leaders in Great Commandment principles, seeking to equip leaders with relational skills so they might lead as Jesus led.

The Galatians 6:6 Retreat Ministry – This ministry offers a unique two-day retreat for ministers and their spouses for personal renewal and for reestablishing and affirming ministry and family priorities.

The Center for Relational Care (CRC) – The CRC provides therapy and support to relationships in crisis through an accelerated process of growth and healing, including Relational Care Intensives for couples, families, and singles.

For more information on how you, your church, ministry, denomination, or movement can be served by the Great Commandment Network write or call:

Great Commandment Network
2511 South Lakeline Blvd.
Cedar Park, Texas 78613
#800-881-8008

Or visit our website: GreatCommandment.net

APPENDIX 3

A SPIRIT-EMPOWERED FAITH

Expresses Itself in Great Commission Living Empowered by Great Commandment Love

begins with the end in mind: The Great Commission calls us to make disciples.

"Go therefore and make disciples of all the nations, baptizing them in the name of the Father and the Son and the Holy Spirit teaching them to observe all that I have commanded you; and lo, I am with you always, even to the end of the age" (Matthew 28:19–20 NASB).

The ultimate goal of our faith journey is to relate to the person of Jesus because it is our relational connection to Jesus that will produce Christlikeness and spiritual growth. This relational perspective of discipleship is required if we hope to have a faith that is marked by the Spirit's power.

Models of discipleship that are based solely upon what we know and what we do are incomplete, lacking the empowerment of a life of loving and living intimately with Jesus. A Spirit-empowered faith is relational and impossible to realize apart from a special work of the Spirit. For example, the Spirit-empowered outcome of "listening to and hearing God" implies relationship—it is both relational in focus and requires the Holy Spirit's power to live.

begins at the right place: The Great Commandment calls us to start with loving God and loving others.

"'You shall love the Lord your God with all your heart, with all your soul, and with all your mind.' This is the first and foremost commandment. The second is like it: 'You shall love your neighbor as yourself.' On these two commandments depend the whole Law and the Prophets" (Matthew 22:37–40 NASB).

Relevant discipleship does not begin with doctrines or teaching, parables or stewardship—but with loving the Lord with all your heart, mind, soul, and strength and then loving the people closest to you. Since Matthew 22:37–40 gives us the first and greatest commandment, a Spirit-empowered faith starts where the Great Commandment tells us to start: A disciple must first learn to deeply love the Lord and to express his love to the "nearest ones"—his or her family, church, and community (and in that order).

embraces a relational process of Christlikeness.

"Walk while you have the light, lest darkness overtake you" (John 12:35 *ESV*).

Scripture reminds us that there are three sources of light for our journey: Jesus, his Word, and his people. The process of discipleship (or becoming more like Jesus) occurs as we relate intimately with each source of light.

Spirit-empowered discipleship will require a lifestyle of:

- Fresh encounters with Jesus (John 8:12)

- Frequent experiences of Scripture (Psalm 119:105)

- Faithful engagement with God's people (Matthew 5:14)

can be defined with observable outcomes using a biblical framework.

"And He Himself gave some to be apostles, some prophets, some evangelists, and some pastors and teachers, for the equipping of the saints for the work of ministry, for the edifying of the body of Christ" (Ephesians 4:11–12 NKJV).

The metrics for measuring Spirit-empowered faith or the growth of a disciple come from Scripture and are organized/framed around four distinct dimensions of a disciple who serves.

A relational framework for organizing Spirit-Empowered Discipleship outcomes draws from a cluster analysis of several Greek (diakoneo, leitourgeo, dou- leuo) and Hebrew words ('abad, Sharat), which elaborate on the Ephesians 4:12 declaration that Christ's followers are to be equipped for works of ministry or service. Therefore, the 40 Spirit Empowered Faith Outcomes have been identified and organized around:

- Serving/loving the Lord – While they were ministering to the Lord and fasting (Acts 13:2 NASB).[1]

- Serving/loving the Word – But we will devote ourselves to prayer and to the ministry of the Word (Acts 6:4 NASB).[2]

- Serving/loving people – Through love serve one another (Galatians 5:13 NASB).[3]

- Serving/loving his mission – Now all these things are from God, who reconciled us to himself through Christ and gave us the ministry of reconciliation (2 Corinthians 5:18 NASB).[4]

---

1   Ferguson, David L. Great Commandment Principle. Cedar Park, Texas: Relationship Press, 2013.
2   Ferguson, David L. Relational Foundations. Cedar Park, Texas: Relationship Press, 2004.
3   Ferguson, David L. Relational Discipleship. Cedar Park, Texas: Relationship Press, 2005.
4   "Spirit Empowered Outcomes," www.empowered21.com, Empowered 21 Global Council, http://empowered21.com/discipleship-materials/.

APPENDIX 4

A SPIRIT-EMPOWERED DISCIPLE LOVES THE LORD THROUGH

L1. Practicing thanksgiving in all things
"Enter the gates with thanksgiving" (Ps. 100:4). "In everything give thanks" (I Th. 5:18). "As sorrowful, yet always rejoicing" (II Cor. 6:10).

L2. Listening to and hearing God for direction and discernment
"Speak Lord, Your servant is listening" (I Sam. 3:8–9). "Mary…listening to the Lord's word, seated at his feet" (Lk.10:38–42). "Shall I not share with Abraham what I am about to do?" (Gen. 18:17). "His anointing teaches you all things" (I Jn. 2:27).

L3. Experiencing God as he really is through deepened intimacy with him
"Hear, O Israel: The Lord our God, the Lord is one. Love the Lord your God with all your heart and with all your soul and with all your strength" (Deut. 6:4,5). "Yet the Lord longs to be gracious to you; therefore he will rise up to show you compassion. For the Lord is a God of justice" (Is. 30:18). See also John 14:9.

L4. Rejoicing regularly in my identity as "His Beloved"
"And His banner over me is love" (Song of Sol. 2:4). "To the praise of the glory of His grace, which He freely bestowed on us in the beloved" (Eph. 1:6). "For the Lord gives to His beloved even in their sleep" (Ps. 127:2).

L5. Living with a passionate longing for purity and to please him in all things
"Who may ascend the hill of the Lord—he who has clean hands and a pure heart" (Ps. 24:3). "Beloved, let us cleanse ourselves from all of flesh and spirit, perfecting holiness in the fear of God" (II Cor. 7:1). "I always do the things that are pleasing to Him" (Jn. 8:29). "Though He slay me, yet will I hope in Him" (Job 13:15).

L6. Consistent practice of self-denial, fasting, and solitude rest
"He turned and said to Peter, '"Get behind me, Satan! You are an obstacle to me. You are thinking not as God does, but as human beings do'" (Matt. 16:23). "But you when you fast…" (Mt. 6:17). "Be still and know that I am God" (Ps. 46:10).

L7. Entering often into Spirit-led praise and worship
"Bless the Lord O my soul and all that is within me…" (Ps. 103:1). "Worship the Lord with reverence" (Ps. 2:11). "I praise Thee O Father, Lord of heaven and earth…" (Mt. 11:25).

L8. **Disciplined, bold and believing prayer**
"Pray at all times in the Spirit" (Eph. 6:18). "Call unto me and I will answer…" (Jer. 33:3)).
"If you ask according to His will—He hears—and you will have…" (I Jn. 5: 14–15).

L9. **Yielding to the Spirit's fullness as life in the Spirit brings supernatural intimacy with the Lord, manifestation of divine gifts, and witness of the fruit of the Spirit**
"For by one Spirit we were all baptized into one body, whether Jews or Greeks, whether slaves or free, and we were all made to drink of one Spirit" (I Cor. 12:13). "You shall receive power when the Holy Spirit comes upon you" (Acts 1:8). "But to each one is given the manifestation of the Spirit for the common good" (I Cor. 12:7). See also, I Pet. 4:10, and Rom. 12:6.

L10. **Practicing the presence of the Lord, yielding to the Spirit's work of Christlikeness**
"And we who with unveiled faces all reflect the Lord's glory, are being transformed into His likeness from glory to glory which comes from the Lord, who is the Spirit" (II Cor. 3:18). "As the deer pants after the water brooks, so my soul pants after You, O God" (Ps. 42:1).

A SPIRIT-EMPOWERED DISCIPLE LIVES THE WORD THROUGH

W1. **Frequently being led by the Spirit into deeper love for the One who wrote the Word**
"Love the Lord thy God—love thy neighbor; upon these two commandments deepens all the law and prophets" (Mt. 22:37-40). "I delight in Your commands because I love them." (Ps. 119:47). "The ordinances of the Lord are pure—they are more precious than gold— sweeter than honey" (Ps. 19:9-10).

W2. **Being a "living epistle" in reverence and awe as his Word becomes real in my life, vocation, and calling**
"You yourselves are our letter—known and read by all men" (II Cor. 3:2). "And the Word became flesh and dwelt among us" (Jn. 1:14). "Husbands love your wives—cleansing her by the washing with water through the Word" (Eph. 5:26). See also Tit. 2:5. "Whatever you do, do your work heartily, as for the Lord…" (Col. 3:23).

W3. **Yielding to the Scripture's protective cautions and transforming power to bring life change in me**
"I gain understanding from Your precepts; therefore I hate every wrong path" (Ps. 119:104). "Be it done unto me according to Your word" (Lk. 1:38). "How can a young man keep his way pure? By living according to Your word" (Ps. 119:9). See also Col. 3:16–17.

W4. **Humbly and vulnerably sharing of the Spirit's transforming work through the Word**
"I will speak of your statutes before kings and will not be put to shame" (Ps. 119:46). "Preach the word; be ready in season and out to shame" (II Tim. 4:2).

W5. Meditating consistently on more and more of the Word hidden in the heart

"I have hidden Your Word in my heart that I might not sin against You" (Ps. 119:12). "May the words of my mouth and the meditation of my heart be pleasing in Your sight, O Lord, my rock and my redeemer" (Ps. 19:14).

W6. Encountering Jesus in the Word for deepened transformation in Christlikeness

"All of us, gazing with unveiled face on the glory of the Lord, are being transformed into the same image from glory to glory, as from the Lord who is the Spirit" (II Cor. 3:18). "If you abide in Me and My words abide in you, ask whatever you wish, and it will be done for you" (Jn. 15:7). See also Lk. 24:32, Ps. 119:136, and II Cor. 1:20.

W7. A life-explained as one of "experiencing Scripture"

"This is that spoken of by the prophets" (Acts 2:16). "My comfort in my suffering is this: Your promise preserves my life" (Ps. 119:50). "My soul is consumed with longing for Your laws at all times" (Ps. 119:20).

W8. Living "naturally supernatural", in all of life, as his Spirit makes the written Word *(logos)* the living Word *(Rhema)*

"Faith comes by hearing and hearing by the Word (Rhema) of Christ" (Rom. 10:17). "Your Word is a lamp to my feet and a light for my path" (Ps. 119:105).

W9. Living abundantly "in the present" as his Word brings healing to hurt and anger, guilt, fear and condemnation—which are *heart hindrances* to life abundant

"The thief comes to steal, kill and destroy…" (John 10:10). "I run in the path of Your commands for You have set my heart free" (Ps. 119:32). "…and you shall know the truth and the truth shall set you free" (Jn. 8:32). "For freedom Christ set us free; so stand firm and do not submit again to the yoke of slavery" (Gal. 5:1).

W10. Implicit, unwavering trust that his Word will never fail

"The grass withers and the flower fades but the Word of God abides forever" (Is. 40:8). "So will My word be which goes forth from My mouth, it will not return to me empty" (Is. 55:11).

A SPIRIT-EMPOWERED DISCIPLE LOVES PEOPLE THROUGH

P1. **Living a Spirit-led life of doing good in all of life: relationships and vocation, community and calling**
"…He went about doing good…" (Acts 10:38). "Let your light shine before men in such a way that they may see your good works, and glorify your Father who is in heaven" (Mt. 5:16). "But love your enemies, and do good, and lend, expecting nothing in return, and your reward will be great, and you will be sons of the Most High; for He Himself is kind to ungrateful and evil men" (Lk. 6:35). See also Rom. 15:2.

P2. **Startling people with loving initiatives to give *first***
"Give, and it will be given to you. They will pour into your lap a good measure—pressed down, shaken together, and running over. For by your standard of measure it will be measured to you in return" (Lk. 6:38). "But Jesus was saying, 'Father, forgive them; for they do not know what they are doing.' (Lk. 23:34). See also Lk. 23:43 and Jn. 19:27.

P3. **Discerning the relational needs of others with a heart to give of his love**
"Let no unwholesome word proceed from your mouth, but only such a word as is good for edification according to the need of the moment, so that it will give grace to those who hear" (Eph. 4:29). "And my God will supply all your needs according to His riches in glory in Christ Jesus" (Phil. 4:19). See also Lk. 6:30.

P4. **Seeing people as needing BOTH redemption from sin AND intimacy in relationships, addressing both human fallenness and aloneness**
"But God demonstrates His own love toward us, in that while we were yet sinners, Christ died for us" (Rom. 5:8). "When Jesus came to the place, He looked up and said to him, 'Zaccheus, hurry and come down, for today I must stay at your house'" (Lk. 19:5). See also Mk. 8:24 and Gen. 2:18.

P5. **Ministering his life and love to our *nearest ones* at home and with family as well as faithful engagement in his Body, the church**
"You husbands in the same way, live with your wives in an understanding way, as with someone weaker, since she is a woman; and show her honor as a fellow heir of the grace of life, so that your prayers will not be hindered" (I Pet. 3:7). See also I Pet. 3:1 and Ps. 127:3.

P6. **Expressing the fruit of the Spirit as a lifestyle and identity**
"But the fruit of the Spirit is love, joy, peace, patience, kindness, goodness, faithfulness, gentleness, self-control…" (Gal. 5:22-23). "With the fruit of a man's mouth his stomach will be satisfied; He will be satisfied with the product of his lips" (Prov. 18:20).

P7. **Expecting and demonstrating the supernatural as his spiritual gifts are made manifest and his grace is at work by his Spirit**
"In the power of signs and wonders, in the power of the Spirit; so that from Jerusalem and round about as far as Illyricum I have fully preached the gospel of Christ" (Rom. 15:19). "Truly, truly, I say to you, he who believes in Me, the works that I do, he will do also…" (Jn. 14:12). See also I Cor. 14:1.

P8. **Taking courageous initiative as a peacemaker, reconciling relationships along life's journey**
"…Live in peace with one another" (I Th. 5:13). "For He Himself is our peace, who made both groups into one and broke down the barrier of the dividing wall" (Eph. 2:14). "Therefore, confess your sins to one another, and pray for one another so that you may be healed. See also Jas. 5:16 and Eph. 4:31–32.

P9. **Demonstrating his love to an ever growing network of "others" as he continues to challenge us to love "beyond our comfort"**
"The one who says, 'I have come to know Him,' and does not keep His commandments, is a liar, and the truth is not in him" (I Jn. 2:4). "If someone says, 'I love God,' and hates his brother, he is a liar; for the one who does not love his brother whom he has seen, cannot love God whom he has not seen" (I Jn. 4:20).

P10. **Humbly acknowledging to the Lord, ourselves, and others that it is Jesus in and through us who is loving others at their point of need**
"Take My yoke upon you and learn from Me, for I am gentle and humble in heart, and you will find rest for your souls" (Mt. 11:29). "If I then, the Lord and the Teacher, washed your feet, you also ought to wash one another's feet" (Jn. 13:14).

A SPIRIT-EMPOWERED DISCIPLE LIVES HIS MISSION THROUGH

M1. **Imparting the gospel and one's very life in daily activities and relationships, vocation and community**
"Having so fond an affection for you, we were well-pleased to impart to you not only the gospel of God but also our own lives, because you had become very dear to us" (I Th. 2:8-9). See also Eph. 6:19.

M2. **Expressing and extending the Kingdom of God as compassion, justice, love, and forgiveness are shared**
"I must preach the kingdom of God to the other cities also, for I was sent for this purpose'" (Lk. 4:43). "As You sent Me into the world, I also have sent them into the world"(Jn. 17:18). "Restore to me the joy of Your salvation and sustain me with a willing spirit. Then I will teach transgressors Your ways, and sinners will be converted to you" (Ps. 51:12–13). See also Mic. 6:8.

M3. **Championing Jesus as the only hope of eternal life and abundant living**
"There is no salvation through anyone else, nor is there any other name under heaven given to the human race by which we are to be saved" (Acts 4:12). "A thief comes only to steal and slaughter and destroy; I came so that they might have life and have it more abundantly" (Jn. 10:10). See also Acts 4:12, Jn. 10:10, and Jn. 14:6.

M4. **Yielding to the Spirit's role to convict others as he chooses, resisting expressions of condemnation**
"And He, when He comes, will convict the world concerning sin and righteousness and judgment…" (Jn. 16:8). "Who is the one who condemns? Christ Jesus is He who died, yes, rather who was raised, who is at the right hand of God, who also intercedes for us" (Rom. 8:34). See also Rom. 8:1.

M5. Ministering his life and love to the "least of these"
"Then He will answer them, 'Truly I say to you, to the extent that you did not do it to one of the least of these, you did not do it to Me'" (Mt. 25:45). "Pure and undefiled religion in the sight of our God and Father is this: to visit orphans and widows in their distress, and to keep oneself unstained by the world" (Jas. 1:27).

M6. Bearing witness of a confident peace and expectant hope in God's Lordship in all things
"Now may the Lord of peace Himself continually grant you peace in every circumstance. The Lord be with you all!" (II Thess. 3:16). "Let the peace of Christ rule in your hearts, to which indeed you were called in one body; and be thankful" (Col. 3:15). See also Rom. 8:28 and Ps. 146:5.

M7. Faithfully sharing of time, talent, gifts, and resources in furthering his mission
"Of this church I was made a minister according to the stewardship from God bestowed on me for your benefit, so that I might fully carry out the preaching of the word of God" (Col. 1:25). "From everyone who has been given much, much will be required; and to whom they entrusted much, of him they will ask all the more" (Lk. 12:48). See also I Cor. 4:1–2.

M8. Attentive listening to others' *story*, vulnerably sharing of our story, and a sensitive witness of Jesus' story as life's ultimate hope; developing your story of prodigal, pre-occupied and pain-filled living; listening for other's story and sharing Jesus' story
"…but sanctify Christ as Lord in your hearts, always being ready to make a defense to everyone who asks you to give an account for the hope that is in you, yet with gentleness and reverence" (I Pet. 3:15). "…because this son of mine was dead, and has come to life again" (Luke 11:24). (Mark 5:21–42). (Jn. 9:1–35).

M9. Pouring our life into others, making disciples who in turn make disciples of others
"Go therefore and make disciples of all nations, baptizing them in the name of the Father and the Son and the Holy Spirit, teaching them to observe all that I commanded you; and lo, I am with you always, even to the end of the age" (Mt. 28:19–20). See also II Tim. 2:2.

M10. Living submissively within his Body, the Church, as instruction and encouragement, reproof and correction are graciously received by faithful disciples
"…and be subject to one another in the fear of Christ" (Eph. 5:21). "Brethren, even if anyone is caught in any trespass, you who are spiritual, restore such a one in a spirit of gentleness; each one looking to yourself, so that you too will not be tempted" (Gal. 6:1). See also Gal. 6:2.

About the Authors

Steve and Barbara Uhlmann are founders and the heartbeat behind the Agape Project, LoveLikeJesus.com, The Intentional Community, and the *Called 2 Love* Initiative. After a financially successful career in the global plastics industry, Steve and Barbara came to the realization they were married yet emotionally alone. Ghosts from the past and a health crisis in the present could have marked the end of it all. Instead, it marked a new and wonderful beginning. Their journey from emotional woundedness to wholeness shows all of us how we can experience an ongoing relational intimacy with the one we love. The Uhlmann's have two adult children, six grandchildren, and two great grandchildren. They reside in Scottsdale, Arizona.

Dr. David and Teresa Ferguson have labored together on behalf of marriage intimacy as God intended for more than forty years. Through the Great Commandment Network, they serve more than twenty denominations and parachurch ministries through pastoral care, training strategies, and resource development. In addition to authoring numerous books, David and Teresa have trained thousands of pastor and ministry leader couples in more than fifty countries of the World with active training network across the US and in Europe, South America, Africa, Asia, and the Middle East. They have three adult children, seven special grandchildren, and two great-grandchildren. They reside in Austin, Texas.

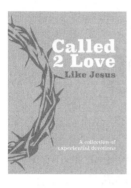

Called 2 Love

Like Jesus

An anthology of teachings and practical exercises from notable followers of Jesus.

Explore the transforming power of your call to love *"as you have been loved."* Also included are practical disciplines to deepen your love of the Lord followed by loving family, friends, and those who need Jesus.

Called 2 Love

The Uhlmann Story

One couple's journey from a mere existence to deepened marriage intimacy.

Married for more than 50 years, Steve and Barbara continue to see relationships as the way to reveal Jesus to the people around us. In their new book, *Called2Love: The Uhlmann Story*, they share the principles of love and change that transformed their lives.

Another Relationship Resource

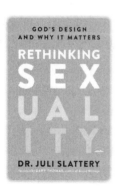

Can Christians reclaim sexuality in a broken culture? We say yes. *Rethinking Sexuality* challenges the paradigm of how Christians have traditionally approached conversations and questions about sexuality. *Rethinking Sexuality* is not just a book but also a movement to equip the Church in addressing biblical sexuality.

Visit: authenticintimacy.com/rethinking to order and to receive a free sample chapter.

Order at: **GreatCommandment.net/resources**